Chinese
Phrases
FOR
DUMMIES

by Dr. Wendy Abraham

WILEY

Wiley Publishing, Inc.

Chinese Phrases For Dummies®

Published by
Wiley Publishing, Inc.
111 River St.
Hoboken, NJ 07030-5774
www.wiley.com

About the Author

Wendy Abraham is the Associate Director of the Stanford Center for Buddhist Studies and the Asian Religions & Cultures Initiative. She has taught courses on Chinese language, Chinese literature, and Asian cultures at Hunter College, Georgetown University, New York University, and Stanford University, where she's currently pursuing her second doctorate in modern Chinese literature. She spent a year researching Shang Dynasty oracle bones in Taiwan, which sparked her deep interest in the development of China's written language. Wendy has directed Chinese language programs for American students in Beijing and Shanghai and has interpreted for high-level arts delegations from China. Her first doctoral dissertation from Teachers College (Columbia University) was on the Chinese Jews of Kaifeng, a subject about which she has written widely and continues to lecture frequently throughout the United States. She also created Jewish Historical Tours of China, bringing people to visit Shanghai and Kaifeng on educational trips. Her interest in all things Chinese continues unabated.

Publisher's Acknowledgments

We're proud of this book; please send us your comments through our Dummies online registration form located at www.dummies.com/register/.

Some of the people who helped bring this book to market include the following:

Acquisitions, Editorial, and Media Development

Compiler: Laura Peterson-Nussbaum

Senior Project Editor: Tim Gallan

Acquisitions Editor: Stacy Kennedy

Copy Editor: Chad R. Sievers

Technical Editor: Wen Yang

Editorial Manager: Christine Meloy Beck

Editorial Assistants: Courtney Allen, Nadine Bell

Cartoons: Rich Tennant, www.the5thwave.com

Composition

Project Coordinators: Adrienne Martinez, Shannon Schiller

Layout and Graphics: Denny Hager, Stephanie D. Jumper, Heather Ryan, Erin Zeltner

Proofreaders: David Faust, Leeann Harney, Joe Niesen, Mildred Rosenzweig

Indexer: Johnna Van Hoose

Publishing and Editorial for Consumer Dummies

Diane Graves Steele, Vice President and Publisher, Consumer Dummies

Joyce Pepple, Acquisitions Director, Consumer Dummies

Kristin A. Cocks, Product Development Director, Consumer Dummies

Michael Spring, Vice President and Publisher, Travel

Kelly Regan, Editorial Director, Travel

Publishing for Technology Dummies

Andy Cummings, Vice President and Publisher, Dummies Technology/General User

Composition Services

Gerry Fahey, Vice President of Production Services

Debbie Stailey, Director of Composition Services

Table of Contents

The 5th Wave

By Rich Tennant

©RICHTENNANT

"You mean, 'wo', 'ta', 'baba', and 'mama' are all words in the Mandarin dialect? My gosh, Alice, our baby's been speaking Chinese the last few weeks!"

Introduction

● ●

Globalization has made familiarity with other people, cultures, and languages not only preferable in the 21st century, but also essential. With the help of the Internet, reaching out and touching someone on the other side of the world has become as easy as the click of a mouse. And yet, nothing quite beats the excitement of a face-to-face encounter with someone who hails from the other side of the globe in his or her own language. Communication in cyberspace doesn't even come close.

Whether you're going around the world for business, getting ready to study overseas, interested in frequenting Chinatown, befriending a Chinese-speaking classmate or coworker, or just plain curious about China, *Chinese Phrases For Dummies* can help you get acquainted with enough Chinese to carry on a decent conversation on any number of topics. You won't become fluent instantly, of course, but this book helps you greet a stranger, buy a plane ticket, order some food, and even adopt a baby. This book also gives you some invaluable cultural tips so that you can not only rattle off those newly acquired words and phrases, but also back them up with the right behavior at the right time.

I design this book to help guide you toward the successful use of one of the most difficult languages on earth. I hope this book makes studying Chinese fun.

About This Book

The good news is that you can use *Chinese Phrases For Dummies* anytime, anywhere. No mandatory class sessions, no exams, and no homework assignments to dread. Need to get to a business meeting after you arrive in a new town? Just turn to the chapter on travel to find out how to haggle for a plane ticket, determine the price, and get to the airport on time. Have to make a sudden trip to the doctor? Turn to the chapter on health and figure out how to tell your caregivers exactly what ails you.

The beauty of this book is that it can basically be all things to all people. You don't have to memorize one chapter before moving on to the next, if what the second chapter deals with what you really need. Read as much or as little as you want, as quickly or as slowly as you like. Whatever interests you is what you can focus on. And remember: You're discovering a language that simultaneously represents one of the world's oldest civilizations and one of today's fastest growing economies.

Note: If you've never taken Chinese before, you may want to read Chapters 1 and 2 before you tackle the later chapters. They give you some of the basics that you need to know about the language, such as how to pronounce the various sounds.

Conventions Used in This Book

Pay attention to a couple of conventions that can help you navigate this book's contents:

- Chinese terms are set in **boldface** to make them stand out.
- Pronunciations and meanings appear in parentheses immediately after the Chinese terms. The pronunciations are in *italics*.

This book uses the *pinyin* (*literally:* spelling the way it sounds) romanization of Chinese words. What does that mean? Well, if you go to China, you see signs in Chinese characters, but if you look for something in English, you may be hard pressed to find it. Whatever signs you see in roman letters are in pinyin, the romanization system developed by the Communists in the 1950s, so seeing pinyin in this book is good practice for you.

Something else to keep in mind as you begin to understand Chinese is that many of the English translations you see in this book aren't exactly literal. Knowing the gist of what you hear or see is more important instead of what individual words in any given phrase mean. For example, if you translate "horse horse tiger tiger" literally into Chinese, you have the phrase meaning "so so." You're not actually talking about animals. Whenever I give a literal translation, I preface it with *"literally"* in italics.

Foolish Assumptions

Some of the foolish assumptions I made about you while writing *Chinese Phrases For Dummies* are

- ✔ You don't know any Chinese, except for maybe a couple of words you picked up from a good kung-fu movie or the word "tofu," which you picked up while grocery shopping.

- ✔ Your goal in life isn't to become an interpreter of Chinese at the United Nations. You just want to pick up some useful words, phrases, and sentence constructions to make yourself understood when speaking Chinese.

- ✔ You have no intention of spending hours and hours memorizing Chinese vocabulary and grammar patterns.

- ✔ You want to have fun while trying to speak a little Chinese, like at your local Chinese restaurant.

Icons Used in This Book

The cute little icons in the left-hand margins highlight the kind of information you're looking at and can help you locate certain types of information in a hurry. This book's five icons are

The bull's-eye appears wherever I highlight a great idea to help make your study of Chinese easier.

This icon serves as a reminder about particularly important information concerning Chinese.

The icon acts as a stop sign in your mind. It warns you something you need to avoid saying or doing so that you don't make a fool of yourself.

This icon clues you in on fascinating bits of information about China and Chinese culture. Knowledge of a culture goes hand in hand with knowledge of a foreign language, so these icons help light the way as you embark on your journey.

This icon highlights various rules of grammar that may be unusual. Even though this book doesn't focus primarily on grammar, by paying attention to these little grammatical rules as they pop up can only enhance your successful execution of the language.

Where to Go from Here

Chinese is often considered one of the toughest languages in the world to master. Don't worry. The good news is that you're not trying to master it. All you want is for people to understand you when you open your mouth. All you have to do now is turn to whichever chapter piques your curiosity and keep practicing your favorite Chinese phrases when you're with your family and friends in Chinatown.

Chapter 1

I Say It How? Speaking Chinese

- -

In This Chapter

▶ Getting a handle on basic Chinese sounds

▶ Perfecting the four basic tones

▶ Practicing Chinese idioms

▶ Understanding basic Chinese phrases and gestures

- -

*T*ime to get your feet wet with the basics of Chinese. This chapter gives you the guidelines that help you pronounce words in standard Mandarin (the official language of both the People's Republic of China and Taiwan) like a native speaker and helps you get a handle on the four tones that distinguish the Mandarin dialect. After you have the basics down, we show you how to construct basic Chinese phrases.

But before you dive in, here's a bit of advice: Don't be intimidated by all the tones! When studying a foreign language, don't worry about making mistakes the minute you open your mouth.

The Written Word: Yikes! No Alphabet!

With so many distinct dialects in Chinese, how do people communicate with each other? The answer lies in . . . (drum roll) . . . the written word.

Say you see two Chinese people sitting next to each other on a train traveling from Canton to Shanghai. If the Cantonese speaker reads the newspaper out loud, the guy from Shanghai won't have a clue what he's saying. But if they both read the same newspaper article silently to themselves, they could understand what's going on in the world. That's because Chinese characters are uniform all across the country.

Chinese words are written in beautiful, often symbolic configurations called *characters*. Each character is a word in and of itself, and sometimes it's a part of a compound word. It makes no difference if you write the characters from right to left, left to right, or top to bottom, because you can read and understand them in any order.

During the Han dynasty, a lexicographer named Xu Shen identified six ways in which Chinese characters reflected meanings and sounds. Of these, four were the most common:

- ✔ **Pictographs:** These characters are formed according to the shape of the objects themselves, such as the sun and the moon.

- ✔ **Ideographs:** These characters represent more abstract concepts. For example, the characters for "above" and "below" each have a horizontal line representing the horizon and another stroke leading out away above or below the horizon.

- ✔ **Complex ideographs:** Combinations of simpler characters, such as the sun and moon together which mean "bright."

> ✔ **Phonetic compounds:** Also called *logographs,*
> these compound characters are formed by two
> graphic elements — one hinting at the meaning
> of the word and the other providing a clue to
> the sound. Phonetic compounds account for
> more than 80 percent of all Chinese characters.

No matter which type of character you see, you won't
find any letters stringing them together like you see in
English. So how in the world do Chinese people con-
sult a Chinese dictionary? In several different ways.

Because Chinese characters are composed of several
(often many) strokes of the writing brush, one way to
look up a character is by counting the number of
strokes and then looking up the character under the
portion of the dictionary that notes characters by
strokes. But to do so, you have to know which radical
to check under first. Chinese characters have 214
radicals — parts of the character that can help identify what the character may signify, such as three dots
on the left-hand side of the character representing
water. Each radical is itself composed of a certain
number of strokes, so you have to first look up the
radical by the number of strokes it takes to write it,
and after you locate that radical, you start looking
once more under the number of strokes left in the
character *after* that radical to locate the character
you wanted to look up in the first place.

You can always just check under the pronunciation of
the character (if you already know how to pronounce
it), but you have to sift through every single character with the same pronunciation first, according to
which tone the word is spoken with — first, second,
third, or fourth. And because Chinese has so many
homophones, this task isn't as easy as it may sound
(no pun intended). For example the word pronounced
"ma" if spoken with a first tone, means "mother," with
a second tone it means "hemp," with a third tone it
means "horse," and with a fourth tone it means "to
scold." So if you're not careful you can scold your
mother and call her a horse.

I bet you feel really relieved that you're only focusing on spoken Chinese and not the written language about now.

Pinyin Spelling: Beijing, Not Peking

To spell the way it sounds . . . that's the literal meaning of **pīnyīn**. For decades, Chinese had been transliterated in any number of ways. Finally, in 1979, the People's Republic of China officially adopted **pīnyīn** as its official romanization system. After the adoption, U.S. libraries and government agencies diligently changed all their prior records from other romanization systems into **pīnyīn**.

Keep in mind the following quick facts about some of the initial sounds in Mandarin when you see them written in the relatively new **pīnyīn** system:

- ✔ **J:** Sounds like the "g" in "gee whiz." An "i" often follows a "j." "**Jǐ kuài qián?**" (*jee kwye chyan*) means "How much money?"

- ✔ **Q:** Sounds like the "ch" in "cheek." You never see it followed by a "u" like in English, but an "i" always follows it in **pīnyīn**, possibly before another vowel or a consonant. **Qīngdǎo** (*cheeng daow*) beer used to be spelled "ch'ing tao" or "Tsingtao."

- ✔ **X:** The third letter that's often followed by an "i." It sounds like the "sh" in "she." One famous Chinese leader, **Dèng Xiǎopíng** (*dung shyaow peeng*), boasted this letter in his name.

- ✔ **Zh:** Unlike "j," which often precedes a vowel — making it sound like you're opening your mouth — "zh" is followed by vowels, which make it sound like your mouth is a bit more closed. Take **Zhōu ēnlái** (*joe un lye*), for example, the great statesman of 20th-century China. When you say his name, it sounds like Joe Un-lye.

✔ **Z:** Sounds like a "dz." You see it in the name of the PRC's first leader, **Máo Zédōng** (*maow dzuh doong*), which used to be spelled Mao Tse-tung.

✔ **C:** Pronounced like "ts" in such words as **cài** (*tsye;* food) or **cèsuǒ** (*tsuh swaw;* bathroom).

✔ **B, D, and G:** In the past, the sounds made by these three letters were represented by P, T, and K, respectively, and the corresponding *aspirated* initial sounds (like in the words "pie," "tie," and "kite") were written as "p'," "t'," and "k'." Today, the letters "P," "T," and "K" represent the aspirated sounds.

Sounding Off: Basic Chinese Sounds

Don't worry about sounding like a native speaker the first time you utter a Chinese syllable — after all, who does? But the longer you procrastinate becoming familiar with the basic elements of Chinese words, the greater your fear of this unique language may become.

The main thing to remember about the Chinese language is that each *morpheme* (the smallest unit of meaning in a language) is represented by one syllable, which in turn consists of an initial sound and a final sound, topped off by a tone. This applies to each and every syllable. Without any one of these three components, your words may be incomprehensible to the average Chinese person. For example, the syllable "**mā**" is comprised of the initial "m" and the final "a," and you pronounce it with what's called a first tone. Together, the parts mean "mother." If you substitute the first tone for a third tone, which is written as "**mǎ**," you say the word "horse." The following sections break up the three parts and give each their due.

Starting off with initials

In Chinese, initials always consist of consonants. Table 1-1 lists the initials you encounter in the Chinese language.

Table 1-1	Chinese Initials	
Chinese Letter	*Sound*	*English Example*
b	baw	bore
p	paw	paw
m	maw	more
f	faw	four
d	duh	done
t	tuh	ton
n	nuh	null
l	luh	lull
g	guh	gull
k	kuh	come
h	huh	hunt
j	gee	gee
q	chee	cheat
x	she	she
z	dzuh	"ds" in suds
c	tsuh	"ts" in huts
s	suh	sun
zh	jir	germ
ch	chir	churn
sh	shir	shirt

Chinese Letter	Sound	English Example
r	ir	"er" in bigger
w	wuh	won
y	yuh	yup

The initials **–n**, **-ng,** and **-r** can also appear as finals (see the next section for more on finals), so don't be surprised if you see them there.

Ending with finals

Chinese boasts many more consonants than vowels. In fact, the language has only six vowels all together: **a, o, e, i, u,** and **ü**. If you pronounce the vowels in sequence, your mouth starts off very wide and your tongue starts off very low. Eventually, when you get to **ü**, your mouth becomes much more closed and your tongue ends pretty high. You can also combine the vowels in various ways to form compound vowels. Table 1-2 lists the vowels and some possible combinations.

Table 1-2	Chinese Vowels	
Chinese Vowel	*Sound*	*English Example*
a	ah	hot
ai	i	eye
ao	ow	chow
an	ahn	sonogram
ang	ahng	angst
o	aw	straw
ong	oong	too + ng

(continued)

Table 1-2 *(continued)*

Chinese Vowel	Sound	English Example
ou	oh	oh
e	uh	bush
ei	ay	way
en	un	ton
eng	ung	tongue
er	ar	are
i	ee	tea
ia	ya	gotcha
iao	yaow	meow
ie	yeh	yet
iu	yo	leo
ian	yan	Cheyenne
iang	yahng	y + angst
in	een	seen
ing	eeng	going
iong	yoong	you + ng
u	oo	too
ua	wa	suave
uo	waw	war
ui	way	way
uai	why	why
uan	wan	want
un	one	one
uang	wahng	wan + ng

Chinese Vowel	Sound	English Example
ueng	wung	one + ng
ü	yew	ewe
üe	yweh	you + eh
üan	ywan	you + wan
ün	yewn	you + n

Tone marks in pīnyīn always appear above the vowel, but if you see a couple of vowels in a row, the tone mark appears above the first vowel in that sequence. One exception is when you see the vowels **iu** and **ui** together. In that case, the tone marks fall on the second vowel.

Sometimes vowels appear without initial consonant accompaniment, but they still mean something. The word **ǎi**, meaning "short" (of stature), is one example.

Perfect pitch: Presenting . . . the four tones

Mandarin has only four tones. The best way to imagine what each of the four tones sounds like is to visualize these short descriptions:

- ✔ **First tone:** High level. The first tone is supposed to be as high as your individual pitch range can be, without wavering. It appears like this above the letter a: **ā**.

- ✔ **Second tone:** Rising. The second tone sounds like you're asking a question. It goes from the middle level of your voice to the top. It doesn't automatically indicate that you're asking a question, however — it just sounds like you are. You mark it like this: **á**.

- ✔ **Third tone:** Falling and then rising. The third tone starts in the middle level of your voice range and then falls deeply before slightly rising at the end. It looks like this if you were to see it above the letter a: **ă**

✔ **Fourth tone:** Falling. The fourth tone sounds like you're giving someone an order (unlike the more plaintive-sounding second tone). It falls from the high pitch level it starts at. Here's how it looks above the letter a: **à**.

Even though tones reduce the number of *homophones* (words that are pronounced alike even if they differ in spelling, meaning, or origin), any given syllable with a specific tone can have more than one meaning. Sometimes the only way to decipher the intended meaning is to see the written word.

One third tone after another

When you have to say a third tone followed by another third tone out loud in consecutive fashion, the first one actually becomes a second tone. If you hear someone say "**Tā hěn hǎo**" (*tah hun how;* she's very well), you may not realize that both "**hěn**" and "**hǎo**" individually are third tone syllables. It sounds like "**hén**" is a second tone and "**hǎo**" is a full third tone.

Half-third tones

Whenever a third tone is followed by any of the other tones — first, second, fourth, or even a neutral tone — it becomes a *half-third tone.* You only pronounce the first half of the tone — the falling half — before you pronounce the other syllables with the other tones. In fact, a half-third tone barely falls at all. It sounds more like a level low tone (kind of the opposite of the high level first tone). Get it?

Neutral tones

A fifth tone exists that you can't exactly count among the four basic tones, because it's actually toneless, or neutral. You never see a tone mark over a fifth tone, and you only say it when you attach it to grammatical particles or the second character of repetitive sylla-bles, such as **bàba** (*bah bah;* father) or **māma** (*mah mah;* mother).

Tonal changes in yī and bù

Just when you think you're getting a handle on all the possible tones and tone changes in Chinese, I have one more aspect to report: The words **yī** (*ee;* one) and **bù** (*boo;* not or no) are truly unusual in Chinese, in that their tones may change automatically depending on what comes after them. You pronounce **yī** by itself with the first tone. However, when a first, second, or third tone follows it, it instantly turns into a fourth tone, such as in **yìzhāng zhě** (*ee jahng jir;* a piece of paper). If a fourth tone follows **yī**, however, it auto-matically becomes a second tone, such as in the word **yíyàng** (*ee yahng;* the same). I know this all sounds very complicated, but when you get the hang of tones, pronunciation becomes second nature. These concepts will sink in quicker than you expect.

Adding Idioms and Popular Expressions to Your Repertoire

The Chinese language has thousands of idiomatic expressions known as **chéngyǔ** (*chung yew*). Most of these **chéngyǔ** originated in anecdotes, fables, fairy tales, or ancient literary works, and some of the expressions are thousands of years old. The vast majority consists of four characters, succinctly expressing morals behind very long, ancient stories. Others are more than four characters. Either way, the Chinese pepper these pithy expressions throughout any given conversation.

Here are a few **chéngyǔ** you frequently hear in Chinese:

- ✔ **Ān bù jiù bān.** (*ahn boo jyoe bahn;* To take one step at a time.)

- ✔ **Huǒ shàng jiā yóu.** (*hwaw shahng jyah yo;* To add fuel to the fire; to aggravate the problem.)

✔ **Hú shuō bā dào.** (*hoo shwaw bah daow; literally:* to talk nonsense in eight directions.) To talk nonsense.

✔ **Mò míng qí miào.** (*maw meeng chee meow; literally:* No one can explain the wonder and mystery of it all.) This saying describes anything that's tough to figure out, including unusual behavior.

✔ **Quán xīn quán yì.** (*chwan sheen chwan ee; literally:* entire heart, entire mind.) Wholeheartedly.

✔ **Rù xiāng suí sú.** (*roo shyahng sway soo;* When in Rome, do as the Romans do.)

✔ **Yì jǔ liǎng dé.** (*ee jyew lyahng duh;* To kill two birds with one stone.)

✔ **Yì mó yì yàng.** (*ee maw ee yahng;* Exactly alike.)

✔ **Yě shēn zuò zé.** (*ee shun dzwaw dzuh;* To set a good example.)

✔ **Yì zhēn jiàn xiě.** (*ee jun jyan shyeh;* To hit the nail on the head.)

Another fact you quickly become aware of when you start speaking with **chéngyǔ** is that the expressions are sometimes full of references to animals. Here are some of those:

✔ **gǒu zhàng rén shì** (*go jahng run shir; literally:* the dog acts fierce when his master is present; to take advantage of one's connections with powerful people)

✔ **guà yáng tóu mài gǒu ròu** (*gwah yahng toe my go roe; literally:* to display a lamb's head but sell dog meat; to cheat others with false claims)

✔ **dǎ cǎo jǐng shé** (*dah tsaow jeeng shuh; literally:* to beat the grass to frighten the snake; to give a warning)

✔ **duì niú tán qín** (*dway nyo tahn cheen; literally:* to play music to a cow; to cast pearls before swine)

✔ **xuán yá lè mǎ** (*shywan yah luh mah; literally:* to rein in the horse before it goes over the edge; to halt)

✔ **huà shé tiān zú** (*hwah shuh tyan dzoo; literally:* to paint a snake and add legs; to gild the lily; to do something superfluous)

✔ **hǔ tóu shé wěi** (*hoo toe shuh way; literally:* with the head of a tiger but the tail of a snake; to start strong but end poorly)

✔ **chē shuǐ mǎ lóng** (*chuh shway mah loong; literally:* cars flowing like water and horses creating a solid line looking like a dragon; heavy traffic)

Mastering Basic Phrases

If you make it a habit to use the following short Chinese phrases whenever you get the chance, you can master them in no time:

✔ **Nǐ hǎo!** (*nee how;* Hi; How are you?)

✔ **Xièxiè.** (*shyeh shyeh;* Thank you.)

✔ **Bú kèqì.** (*boo kuh chee;* You're welcome; Don't mention it.)

✔ **Méi shì.** (*may shir;* It's nothing; Don't mention it.)

✔ **Hǎo jíle.** (*how jee luh;* Great; Fantastic.)

✔ **Duì le.** (*dway luh;* That's right.)

✔ **Gōngxǐ gōngxǐ!** (*goong she goong she;* Congratulations!)

✔ **Duìbuqǐ.** (*dway boo chee;* Excuse me.)

✔ **Suàn le.** (*swan luh;* Forget it; Never mind.)

✔ **Méiyǒu guānxi.** (*mayo gwan she;* It doesn't matter.)

✔ **Děng yíxià.** (*dung ee shyah;* Wait a minute.)

Communicating with body language

Ever think you know what certain couples are saying or thinking just by observing their gestures and body language? Well, people can make the same observations in China. Although the gestures are different, they contain important clues as to social status between people, their emotions, and so on. Observe Chinese people wherever you can to see if you notice any of the following gestures:

- ✔ **Pointing to one's own nose.** You may find this hard to believe, but Chinese people often point to their own noses, often touching them, when they refer to themselves by saying the word "**wŏ**" (*waw;* I). The Chinese are probably just as curious as to why Westerners point to their hearts.

- ✔ **Nodding and bowing slightly.** When greeting older people, professors, or others in positions of power or prestige, people lower their heads slightly to acknowledge them and show respect. Unlike the Japanese, who bow deeply, the Chinese basically bow with their heads in a slight fashion.

- ✔ **Shaking hands.** People of vastly different status generally don't give each other a handshake, but it's common among friends and business colleagues.

- ✔ **Bowing with hands clasped.** If you see hand clasping and bowing going on at the same time, you know the participants have something to celebrate. It indicates conveying congratulations or greeting others during special festival occasions. Their hands are held at chest level and their heads are slightly bowed (and they often have big smiles on their faces).

Chapter 2

Grammar on a Diet: Just the Basics

In This Chapter

▶ Getting the hang of the parts of speech

▶ Discovering how to ask questions

*Y*ou're probably one of those people who cringe at the mere mention of the word *grammar*. Just the thought of all those rules on how to construct sentences can put you into a cold sweat.

Hey, don't sweat it! This chapter could just as easily be called "Chinese without Tears." It gives you some quick and easy shortcuts on how to combine the basic building blocks of Chinese (which, by the way, are the same components that make up English).

How Chinese Is Easier Than English

The basic word order of Chinese is exactly the same as in English. Just think of it this way: When you say "I love spinach," you're using the subject (I), verb (love), object (spinach) sentence order. It's the same in Chinese. Only in Beijing, it sounds more like **Wǒ xǐhuān bōcài** (*waw she hwahn baw tsye*).

And if that weren't enough to endear you to Chinese already, maybe these tidbits of information will.

- ✔ You don't need to conjugate verbs!
- ✔ You don't need to master verb tenses. (Don't you just love it already?)
- ✔ You don't need to distinguish between singular and plural nouns.
- ✔ You don't need to worry about gender-specific nouns.
- ✔ You can use the same word for both the subject and the object.

The way you can tell how one part of a Chinese sentence relates to another is generally by the use of particles and what form the word order takes. (For those of you presently scratching your heads, you can find particles at the beginning or end of sentences; they serve mainly to distinguish different types of emphatic statements but can't be translated in and of themselves.)

Some interesting characteristics of the Chinese language include

- ✔ You don't have to think about first, second, or third person (for example, "I eat" versus "he eats").
- ✔ You don't have to worry about active or passive voices (for example, "hear" versus "be heard").
- ✔ You don't have to concern yourself with the past or present ("I like him" versus "I liked him").

In addition, Chinese language has only two aspects — complete and continuous — whereas English has all sorts of different aspects: indefinite, continuous, perfect, perfect continuous, and so on. (Examples include ways of distinguishing between "I eat," "I ate," "I will eat," "I said I would eat," "I am eating," and so on.) *Aspects* are what characterize the Chinese language in place of tenses. Aspects refer to how a speaker views an event or state of being.

Naming Those Nouns

Chinese is just chock-full of nouns:

- ✔ Common nouns that represent tangible things, such as **háizi** (*hi dzuh;* child) or **yè** (*yeh;* leaf)

- ✔ Proper nouns for such items as names of countries or people, like **Fǎguó** (*fah gwaw;* France) and **Zhāng Xiānsheng** (*jahng shyan shung;* Mr. Zhang)

- ✔ Material nouns for such nondiscrete things as **kāfēi** (*kah fay;* coffee) or **jīn** (*jin;* gold)

- ✔ Abstract nouns for such items as **zhèngzhì** (*juhng jir;* politics) or **wénhuà** (*one hwah;* culture)

Pronouns

Pronouns are easy to make plural in Chinese. Here's what you need to know: Just add the plural suffix **-men** to the three basic pronouns:

- ✔ **Wǒ** (*waw;* I/me) becomes **wǒmen** (*waw mun;* we/us).

- ✔ **Nǐ** (*nee;* you) becomes **nǐmen** (*nee mun;* you [plural]).

- ✔ **Tā** (*tah;* he/him, she/her, it) becomes **tāmen** (*tah mun;* they/them).

Sometimes instead of using the term **wǒmen** for "us," you'll hear the term **zánmen** instead. This word is used in very familiar settings when the speaker is trying to include the listener in an action, like when you say **Zánmen zǒu ba** (*dzah mun dzoe bah;* let's go).

When speaking to an elder or someone you don't know too well and the person is someone to whom you should show respect, you need to use the pronoun **nín** (*neen*) instead of the more informal **nǐ** (nee). On the other hand, if you're speaking to several people who fit that description, the plural remains **nǐmen** (*nee mun*).

Classifiers

Classifiers, sometimes called measure words, help classify particular nouns. For example, the classifier **běn** (*bun*) can refer to books, magazines, dictionaries, and just about anything else that's printed and bound like a book. You may hear **Wǒ yào yìběn shū** (*waw yaow ee bun shoo;* I want a book.) just as easily as you'll hear **Wǒ yào kàn yìběn zázhì** (*waw yaow kahn ee bun dzah jir;* I want to read a magazine.).

Classifiers are found in between a number (or a demonstrative pronoun such as "this" or "that") and a noun. They're similar to the English words such as "herd" (of elephants) or "school" (of fish).

Because you have so many potential classifiers to choose from in Chinese, the general rule is: When in doubt, use **ge** (*guh*). It's the all-purpose classifier and the one used the most in the Chinese language. Just don't give into the temptation to leave a classifier out altogether because no one may understand you at all.

Table 2-1 lists classifiers for natural objects, but first here are some other examples:

✔ **gēn** (*gun*): Used for anything looking like a stick, such as a string or even a blade of grass

✔ **kē** (*kuh*): Used for anything round and tiny, such as a pearl

✔ **zhāng** (*jahng*): Used for anything with a flat surface, such as a newspaper, table, or bed

Table 2-1		Some Typical Classifiers for Natural Objects
Classifier	*Pronunciation*	*Used For*
duǒ	dwaw	flowers
kē	kuh	trees
lì	lee	grain (of rice, sand, and so on)
zhī	jir	animals, insects, birds
zuò	dzwaw	hills, mountains

Whenever you have a pair of anything, you can use the classifier **shuāng** (*shwahng*). That goes for **yì shuāng kuàizi** (*ee shwahng kwye dzuh;* a pair of chopsticks) as well as for **yì shuāng shǒu** (*ee shwahng show;* a pair of hands). Sometimes a pair is indicated by the classifier **duì** (*dway*), as in **yí duì ěrhuán** (*ee dway are hwahn;* a pair of earrings).

Singular and plural: It's not an issue

Regular nouns in Chinese make no distinction between singular and plural. Whether you want to talk about one **píngguǒ** (*peeng gwaw;* apple), two **júzi** (*jyew dzuh;* oranges), or both **píngguǒ hé júzi** (*peeng gwaw huh jyew dzuh;* apples and oranges), the fruits always sound the same in Chinese. On the other hand, if you want to refer to human beings, you can always add the suffix **men** (*mun*). The word for "I" or "me" is **wǒ** (*waw*), but "we" becomes **wǒmen** (*waw mun*). The same goes for **nǐ** (*nee;* you) and **tā** (*tah;* he, she, and it). "They" becomes **nǐmen** (*nee mun*) or **tāmen** (*tah mun*). If you want to refer to a specific number of apples, however, you don't use "men" as a suffix. You can either say **píngguǒ** (*peeng gwaw*) for apple (or apples) or **liǎngge píngguǒ** (*lyahng guh peeng gwaw*), meaning two apples. Got it?

Never attach the suffix **-men** to anything not human. People will think you're nuts if you start referring to your two pet cats as **wǒde xiǎo māomen** (*waw duh shyaow maow mun*). Just say **Wǒde xiǎo māo hěn hǎo, xièxiè,** (*waw duh shyaow maow hun how, shyeh shyeh;* My cats are fine, thank you), and that should do the trick.

Those Little Words: Definite Versus Indefinite Articles

If you're looking for those little words "a," "an," and "the" in Chinese, they simply don't exist. The only way you can tell whether something is being referred to specifically (hence, considered definite) or just generally (and therefore it's indefinite) is by the word order. Nouns that refer specifically to something are usually found at the beginning of the sentence, before the verb.

- ✔ **Shū zài nàr.** (*shoo dzye nar;* The book[s] are there.)

- ✔ **Háizimen xǐhuān tā.** (*hi dzuh mun she hwahn tah;* The children like her.)

- ✔ **Pánzi zài zhuōzishàng.** (*pahn dzuh dzye jwaw dzuh shahng;* There's a plate on the table.)

You can often find those articles that refer to something more general (and are therefore "indefinite") at the end of the sentence, after the verb.

- ✔ **Nǎr yǒu huā?** (*nar yo hwah;* Where are there some flowers? *Or,* Where is there a flower?)

- ✔ **Nàr yǒu huā.** (*nar yo hwah;* There are some flowers over there. *Or,* There's a flower over there.)

- ✔ **Zhèige yǒu wèntí.** (*jay guh yo one tee;* There's a problem with this. *Or,* There are some problems with this.)

These rules do have a few exceptions: If you find a noun at the beginning of a sentence, it may refer to something indefinite if the sentence makes a general comment (instead of telling a whole story), like when you see the verb **shì** (*shir;* to be) as part of the comment:

Xióngmāo shì dòngwù. (*shyoong maow shir doong woo;* Pandas are animals.)

You use the same rule if an adjective comes after the noun, such as

Pútáo hěn tián. (*poo taow hun tyan;* Grapes are very sweet.)

Or if there's an auxiliary verb:

Xiǎo māo huì zhuā lǎoshǔ. (*shyaow maow hway jwah laow shoo;* Kittens can catch mice.)

Or a verb indicating that the action occurs habitually:

Niú chī cǎo. (*nyo chir tsaow;* Cows eat grass.)

Nouns that are preceded by a numeral and a classifier, especially when the word **dōu** (*doe;* all) exists in the same breath, are also considered to be definite:

Sìge xuéshēng dōu hěn cōngmíng. (*suh guh shweh shung doe hun tsoong meeng;* The four students are all very smart.)

If the word **yǒu** (*yo;* to exist) comes before the noun and is then followed by a verb, the reference may be indefinite:

Yǒu shū zài zhuōzishàng. (*yo shoo dzye jwaw dzuh shahng;* There are books on top of the table.)

If you see the word **zhè** (*juh;* this) or **nà** (*nah;* that) plus a classifier used when a noun comes after the verb, it indicates a definite reference:

Wǒ yào mǎi nà zhāng huà. (*waw yaow my nah jahng hwah;* I want to buy that painting.)

Describing Adjectives

Adjectives describe nouns — the question is where to put them. The general rule in Chinese is, if the adjective is pronounced with only one syllable, it appears immediately in front of the noun it qualifies. The following are a couple examples:

✔ **lǜ chá** (*lyew chah;* green tea)

✔ **cháng zhītiáo** (*chahng jir tyaow;* long stick)

If the adjective has two syllables, though, the possessive particle **de** (*duh*) comes between it and whatever it's qualifying:

✔ **gānjìng de yīfu** (*gahn jeeng duh ee foo;* clean clothes)

✔ **cāozá de wǎnhuì** (*tsaow dzah duh wahn hway;* noisy party)

And if a numeral is followed by a classifier, they both need to go in front of the adjective and what it's qualifying:

✔ **yí jiàn xīn yīfu** (*ee jyan shin ee foo;* a [piece of] new clothing)

✔ **sān běn yǒuyìsi de shū** (*sahn bun yo ee suh duh shoo;* three interesting books)

One unique thing about Chinese is that when an adjective is also the predicate, appearing at the end of a sentence, it follows the subject or the topic without needing the verb **shì** (*shir;* to be):

✔ **Tā de fángzi hěn gānjìng.** (*tah duh fahng dzuh hun gahn jeeng;* His house [is] very clean.)

✔ **Nà jiàn yīfu tài jiù.** (*nah jyan ee foo tye jyoe;* That piece of clothing [is] too old.)

Verbs

Good news! You never have to worry about conjugating a Chinese verb in your entire life! If you hear someone say **Tāmen chī Yìdàlì fàn** (*tah men chir ee dah lee fahn*), it could mean "They eat Italian food" just as easily as it could mean "They are eating Italian food." Table 2-2 lists some common verbs.

Table 2-2	Some Common Chinese Verbs	
Chinese	*Pronunciation*	*Translation*
chī	chir	to eat
kàn	kahn	to see
mâi	my	to buy
mài	my	to sell
rènshi	run shir	to know (a person)
shì	shir	to be
yào	yaow	to want/to need
yôu	yo	to have
zhīdào	jir daow	to know (a fact)
zôu lù	dzoe loo	to walk
zuò fàn	dzwaw fahn	to cook

Feeling tense? Le, guò, and other aspect markers

Okay, you can relax now. No need to get tense with Chinese because verbs don't indicate tenses all by themselves. That's the job of *aspect markers*. Those are little syllables that indicate whether an action has been completed, is continuing, has just begun, and just about everything in between.

Take the syllable **le** (*luh*), for example. It can indicate an action has been completed if it's used as a suffix to a verb:

> ✔ **Nǐ mǎi le hěn duō shū.** (*nee my luh hun dwaw shoo;* You bought many books.)

> ✔ **Tā dài le tāde yǔsǎn.** (*tah dye luh tah duh yew sahn;* He brought his umbrella.)

And if you want to turn it into a question, just add **méiyǒu** (*mayo*) at the end. It automatically negates the action completed by **le.**

> ✔ **Nǐ mǎi le hěn duō shū méiyǒu?** (*nee my luh hun dwaw shoo mayo;* Have you bought many books? *Or,* Did you buy many books?)

> ✔ **Tā dài le tāde yǔsǎn méiyǒu?** (*tah dye luh tah duh yew sahn mayo;* Did he bring his umbrella?)

Then there's **guò** (*gwaw*). It basically means that something has been done at one point or another even though it's not happening right now:

> ✔ **Tā qù guò Měiguó.** (*ta chyew gwaw may gwaw;* He has been to America.)

> ✔ **Wǒmen chī guò Fǎguó cài.** (*waw mun chir gwaw fah gwaw tsye;* We have eaten French food before.)

If an action is happening just as you speak, you use the aspect marker **zài** (*dzye*):

> ✔ **Wǒmen zài chīfàn.** (*waw mun dzye chir fahn;* We are eating.)

> ✔ **Nǐ māma zài zuòfàn.** (*nee mah mah dzye dzwaw fahn;* Your mother is cooking.)

If something is or was happening continually and resulted from something else you did, just add the syllable **zhe** (*juh*) to the end of the verb and you can say things like

✔ **Tā dài zhe yíge huáng màozi.** (*tah dye juh ee guh hwahng maow dzuh;* He's wearing a yellow hat.)

✔ **Nǐ chuān zhe yí jiàn piàoliàng de chènshān.** (*nee chwan juh ee jyan pyaow lyahng duh ee foo;* You're wearing a pretty shirt.)

Another way you can use **zhe** is when you want to indicate two actions occurring at the same time:

Tā zuò zhe chīfàn. (*tah dzwaw juh chir fahn;* She is/was sitting there eating.)

Coverbs

The coverb **bǎ** often appears right after the subject of the sentence, separating it from the direct object, which is always something concrete rather than an abstract idea. It separates the indirect and direct objects.

Instead of having the following sentence pattern:

Subject + Verb + Complement (+ Indirect Object) + Object

You have:

Subject + **bǎ** + Object + Verb + Complement (+ Indirect Object)

Here are some examples:

✔ **Wǒ bǎ shū jiè gěi nǐ.** (*waw bah shoo jyeh gay nee;* I'll loan you the book.)

✔ **Qǐng nǐ bǎ běnzi ná gěi lǎoshī.** (*cheeng nee bah bun dzuh nah gay laow shir;* Please give the notebook to the teacher.)

You use the coverb **bǎ** (*bah*) when you want to put the object right up front before you state the verb that tells what you did or will do with the object.

To be or not to be: The verb shì

Be careful not to put the verb **shì** (*shir*) in front of an adjective unless you really mean to make an emphatic statement. In the course of normal conversation, you might say **Nà zhǐ bǐ tài guì** (*nah jir bee tye gway;* That pen [is] too expensive). You wouldn't say **Nà zhǐ bǐ shì tài guì** (*nah jir bee shir tye gway*) unless you really meant to say "That pen IS too expensive!" in which case you'd emphasize the word **shì** when saying it, too.

To negate the verb **shì,** put the negative prefix **bù** in front of it. "**Shì bú shì?**" (*shir boo shir;* Is it or isn't it?) and "**Zhè bú shì táng cù yú**" (*jay boo shir tahng tsoo yew;* This isn't sweet and sour fish.) are two examples.

The special verb: Yǒu (to have)

Do you **yǒu** (*yo*) a computer? No?! Too bad. Everyone else seems to have one these days. How about a Ferrari? Do you **yǒu** one of those? If not, welcome to the club. People who have lots of things use the word **yǒu** pretty often. It means "to have."

- ✔ **Wǒ yǒu yí wàn kuài qián.** (*waw yo ee wahn kwye chyan;* I have $10,000.)

- ✔ **Wǒ yǒu sānge fángzi — yíge zài ōuzhōu, yíge zài Yàzhōu, yíge zài Měiguó.** (*waw yo sahn guh fahng dzuh — ee guh dzye oh joe, ee guh dzye yah joe, ee guh dzye may gwaw;* I have three homes — one in Europe, one in Asia, and one in America.)

Another way **yǒu** can be translated is "there is" or "there are":

- ✔ **Yǒu hěn duō háizi.** (*yo hun dwaw hi dzuh;* There are many children.) As opposed to: **Wǒ yǒu hěn duō háizi**. (*waw yo hun dwaw hi dzuh;* I have many children.)

- ✔ **Shūzhuōshàng yǒu wǔ zhāng zhǐ.** (*shoo jwaw shahng yo woo jahng jir;* There are five pieces of paper on the desk.)

To negate the verb **yǒu,** you can't use the usual negative prefix **bù.** Instead, you must use another term indicating negation, **méi:**

✔ **Méiyǒu hěn duō háizi.** (*mayo hun dwaw hi dzuh;* There aren't many children.)

✔ **Shūzhuōshàng méiyǒu wǔ zhāng zhǐ.** (*shoe jwaw shahng may yo woo jahng jir;* There aren't five pieces of paper on the desk.)

Asking for what you want: The verb yào

Yào (*yaow*) is one of the coolest verbs in Chinese. When you say it, you usually get what you want. In fact, the mere mention of the word **yào** means that you want something.

✔ **Wǒ yào yì bēi kāfēi.** (*waw yaow ee bay kah fay;* I want a cup of coffee.)

✔ **Wǒ yào gēn nǐ yìqǐ qù kàn diànyǐng.** (*waw yaow gun nee ee chee chyew kahn dyan yeeng;* I want to go to the movies with you.)

You can also give someone an order with the verb **yào,** but only if you use it with a second-person pronoun:

✔ **Nǐ yào xiǎoxīn!** (*nee yaow shyaow sheen;* You should be careful!)

✔ **Nǐ yào xǐ shǒu.** (*nee yaow she show;* You need to wash your hands.)

Advocating Adverbs

Adverbs serve to modify verbs or adjectives and always appear in front of them. The most common ones you'll find in Chinese are **hěn** (*hun;* very) and **yě** (*yeah;* also).

If you want to say that something isn't just **hǎo** (*how; good*), but that it's *very* good, you say it's **hěn hǎo** (*hun how; very good*). If your friend wants to then put his two cents in and say that something else is also really good, he'd say "**Zhèige yě hěn hǎo**" (*Jay guh yeah hun how; This is also very good.*) because **yě** always comes before **hěn**.

The adverb **yě** always comes not only before the adverb **hěn** but also before the negative prefix **bù**.

Bù and Méiyǒu: Total Negation

Boo! Did I scare you? Don't worry. I'm just being negative in Chinese. That's right, the word **bù** is pronounced the same way a ghost might say it (*boo*) and is often spoken with the same intensity.

Bù can negate something you've done in the past or the present (or at least indicate you don't generally do it these days), and it can also help negate something in the future:

- **Tā xiǎo de shíhòu bù xǐhuān chī shūcài.** (*tah shyaow duh shir ho boo she hwahn chir shoo tsye;* When he was young, he didn't like to eat vegetables.)

- **Wǒ búyào chàng gē.** (*waw boo yaow chahng guh;* I don't want to sing.)

- **Wǒ bú huà huàr.** (*waw boo hwah hwar;* I don't paint.)

- **Diànyǐngyuàn xīngqīliù bù kāimén.** (*dyan yeeng ywan sheeng chee lyo boo kye mun;* The movie theater isn't open on Saturday.)

The negative prefix **bù** is usually spoken with a fourth (falling) tone. However, when it precedes a syllable with another fourth tone, it becomes a second (rising) tone instead, as in such word as **búqù** (*boo chyew; won't/didn't/*

doesn't go) or **búyào** (*boo yaow;* don't/ didn't/won't want). (For more about tones, see Chapter 1.)

Remember that when Chinese people speak quickly, they may leave out the second syllable in a few bisyllabic verbs and even a few auxiliary verbs like in the "verb-**bù**-verb" pattern. So, instead of saying "**Tā xǐhuān bùxǐhuān hē jiǔ?**" (*tah she hwan boo she hwan huh jyo;* Does he or she like to drink wine?), you may hear someone say "**Tā xǐ bùxǐhuān hē jiǔ?**" (*tah she boo she hwan huh jyoe.*).

Méiyǒu is another negative prefix that also goes before a verb. It refers only to the past, though, and means either something didn't happen or at least didn't happen on a particular occasion.

> ✔ **Wǒ méiyǒu kàn nèi bù diànyǐng.** (*waw mayo kahn nay boo dyan yeeng;* I didn't see that movie.)

> ✔ **Zuótiān méiyǒu xiàyǔ.** (*dzwaw tyan mayo shyah yew;* It didn't rain yesterday.)

If the aspect marker **guò** is at the end of the verb **méiyǒu**, it means it never happened (up until now) in the past. By the way, you'll sometimes find that **méiyǒu** is shortened just to **méi**:

> ✔ **Wǒ méi qù guò Fǎguó.** (*waw may chyew gwaw fah gwaw;* I've never been to France.)

> ✔ **Wǒ méi chī guò Yìndù cài.** (*wo may chir gwaw een doo tsye;* I've never eaten Indian food.)

Getting Possessive with the Particle De

The particle **de** is ubiquitous in Chinese. Wherever you turn, there it is. **Wǒde tiān!** (*waw duh tyan;* My goodness!) Using it is easy. All you have to do is

attach it to the end of the pronoun, such as **nǐde chē**
(*nee duh chuh;* your car) or other modifier, such as
tā gōngsǐ de jīnglǐ (*tah goong suh duh jeeng lee;* his
company's manager), and — *voilà* — it indicates
possession.

> **Nǐde diànnǎo yǒu méiyǒu yǐntèwǎng?** (*nee duh
> dyan now yo mayo een tuh wahng;* Does your
> computer have Internet?)

> **Kěxǐ méiyǒu. Nǐde ne?** (*kuh she mayo. nee duh
> nuh;* Unfortunately not. How about yours?)

The particle **de** acts as an apostrophe "s" ('s)
in English when it's not attached to a pronoun. It also makes the process of modifica-
tion exactly the opposite of the French
possessive "de" or the English "of," with
which you may be tempted to compare it.

Asking Questions

You can ask questions in Chinese in a couple easy
ways. You may be so curious about the world around
you that you ask tons of questions after you know how.

The question particle "ma"

By far the easiest way to ask a question is simply to
end any given statement with a **ma**. That automatically makes it into a question. For example, **Tā chīfàn**
(*tah chir fahn;* He's eating/he eats.) becomes **Tā
chīfàn ma?** (*tah chir fahn mah;* Is he/does he eat?). **Nǐ
shuō Zhōngwén** (*nee shwaw joong one;* You speak
Chinese.) becomes **Nǐ shuō Zhōngwén ma?** (*nee
shwaw joong one mah;* Do you speak Chinese?).

Using bù to ask a question

The second way you can ask a question is just to
repeat the verb in its negative form. The English
equivalent would be to say something like "Do you

eat, not eat?" for example. You can use this format only for a yes or no question, though. For example:

✔ **Nǐ shì búshì Zhōngguórén?** (*nee shir boo shir joong gwaw run;* Are you Chinese?)

✔ **Tā yào búyào háizi?** (*tah yaow boo yaow hi dzuh;* Does he want children?)

✔ **Tāmen xǐhuān bùxǐhuān chī Zhōngguó cài?** (*tah mun she hwahn boo she hwahn chir joong gwaw tsye;* Do they like to eat Chinese food?)

Interrogative pronouns

The last way of asking questions in Chinese is to use interrogative pronouns. The following are pronouns that act as questions in Chinese:

✔ **nǎ** (*nah* + classifier; which)

✔ **nǎr** (*nar;* where)

✔ **shéi** (*shay;* who/whom)

✔ **shéi de** (*shay duh;* whose)

✔ **shénme** (*shummuh;* what)

✔ **shénme dìfāng** (*shummuh dee fahng;* where)

Don't confuse **nǎ** with **nǎr**. That one extra letter makes the difference between saying "which" (**nǎ**) and "where" (**nǎr**).

Figuring out where such interrogative pronouns should go in any given sentence is easy. Just put them wherever the answer would be found. For example:

✔ Question: **Nǐ shì shéi?** (*nee shir shay;* Who are you?)

✔ Answer: **Nǐ shì wǒ péngyǒu.** (*nee shir waw puhng yo;* You are my friend.)

✔ Question: **Tāde nǚpéngyǒu zài nǎr?** (*tah duh nyew puhng yo dzye nar;* Where is his girlfriend?)

✔ Answer: **Tāde nǚpéngyǒu zài jiālǐ.** (*tah duh nyuew puhng yo dzye jyah lee;* His girlfriend is at home.)

This rule also goes for the verb-**bù**-verb pattern. All you have to do to answer that type of question is omit either the positive verb or the negative prefix and verb following it:

Question: Nǐ hǎo bù hǎo? (*nee how boo how;* How are you? *Literally:* Are you good or not good?)

Answer: Wǒ hǎo. (*waw how;* I'm okay.). Or **Wǒ bùhǎo.** (*waw boo how;* I'm not okay.).

Chapter 3

Numerical Gumbo: Counting of All Kinds

• •

In This Chapter

▶ Counting to 10

▶ Telling time

▶ Ticking off the calendar

▶ Spending money

• •

*N*umbers make the world go round, or is that money? Well, it's probably both. This chapter gives you a rundown on number and money phrases and also shows you how to tell time and navigate the months of the year.

1, 2, 3: Cardinal Numbers

Cardinal numbers are important when talking about amounts, telling time, or exchanging money. Table 3-1 lists numbers from 1 to 19.

Table 3-1	Numbers from 1 to 19	
Chinese	*Pronunciation*	*Translation*
líng	leeng	0
yī	ee	1
èr	are	2
sān	sahn	3
sì	suh	4
wǔ	woo	5
liù	lyo	6
qī	chee	7
bā	bah	8
jiû	jyoe	9
shí	shir	10
shíyī	shir ee	11 (literally 10 + 1)
shí'èr	shir are	12 (literally 10 + 2)
shísān	shir sahn	13
shísì	shir suh	14
shíwû	shir woo	15
shíliù	shir lyo	16
shíqī	shir chee	17
shíbā	shir bah	18
shíjiǔ	shir jyoe	19

If the number "two" comes before a classifier (see Chapter 2), use the word **liǎng** instead of **èr**. So you would say that you have **liǎng běn shū** (*lyahng bun shoo;* two books) instead of **èr běn shū** (*are bun shoo*).

When you get to 20, you have to literally think "two tens" — plus whatever single digit you want to add to that up until nine for 21 through 29, as shown in Table 3-2.

Table 3-2	Numbers from 20 to 29	
Chinese	*Pronunciation*	*Translation*
èrshí	are shir	20 (literally two tens)
èrshíyī	are shir ee	21 (two tens plus one)
èrshí'èr	are shir are	22
èrshísān	are shir sahn	23
èrshísì	are shir suh	24
èrshíwǔ	are shir woo	25
èrshíliù	are shir lyo	26
èrshíqī	are shir chee	27
èrshíbā	are shir bah	28
èrshíjiǔ	are shir jyoe	29

The same basic idea goes for **sānshí** (*sahn shir;* thirty; *literally:* three tens), **sìshí** (*suh shir;* forty), **wǔshí** (*woo shir;* fifty), **liùshí** (*lyo shir;* sixty), **qīshí** (*chee shir;* seventy), **bāshí** (*bah shir;* eighty) and **jiǔshí** (*jyoe shir;* ninety). What could be easier?

After the number 99, you can no longer count by tens.

- 100 is **yì bǎi** (*ee bye*).
- 1,000 is **yì qiān** (*ee chyan*).
- 10,000 is **yí wàn** (*ee wahn; literally:* one unit of ten thousand).
- 100,000 is **shí wàn** (*shir wahn; literally:* ten units of ten thousand).

✔ 1,000,000 is **yì bǎi wàn** (*ee bye wahn; literally:* one hundred units of 10,000).

✔ 100,000,000 is **yí yì** (*ee ee; one hundred million*).

Chinese people count all the way up to **wàn** (*wahn;* ten thousand) and then repeat up to **yì** (*ee;* a hundred million), unlike in English, where counting goes up to a thousand before being repeated all the way to a million.

Numbers are represented with the higher units of value first. So the number 387 is **sān bǎi bā shí qī** (*sahn bye bah shir chee*). The number 15,492 is **yí wàn wǔ qiān sì bǎi jiǔ shí èr** (*ee wahn woo chyan suh bye jyoe shir are*).

The number 1 (**yī**) changes its tone from its first (high) to the fourth (falling) tone when followed by a first (high) tone as in **yì qiān** (*ee chyan;* 1,000), by a second (rising) tone as in **yì nián** (*ee nyan;* one year), and by a third (low dipping) tone as in **yì bǎi** (*ee bye;* 100). (See Chapter 1 for a review of the four tones.) And it changes to the second (rising) tone when followed by a fourth (falling) tone as in **yí wàn** (*ee wahn;* 10,000). It remains its original first tone mark only when people count numbers: one, two, three, and so on.

If you want to add a half to anything, the word for half is **bàn** (*bahn*), and it can either come at the beginning, such as in **bàn bēi kělè** (*bahn bay kuh luh;* a half a glass of cola), or after a number and classifier but before the object, to mean "and a half," such as in **yí ge bàn xīngqī** (*ee guh bahn sheeng chee;* a week and a half).

Discovering Ordinal Numbers

Ever tell someone to make a right at the second **jiāotōng dēng** (*jyaow toong dung;* traffic light) or that your house is the third one on the left? Creating ordinal numbers in Chinese is quite easy. Just put **dì** in front of the numeral:

- ✔ **dì yī** (*dee ee;* first)
- ✔ **dì èr** (*dee are;* second)
- ✔ **dì sān** (*dee sahn;* third)
- ✔ **dì sì** (*dee suh;* fourth)
- ✔ **dì wǔ** (*dee woo;* fifth)
- ✔ **dì liù** (*dee lyoe;* sixth)
- ✔ **dì qī** (*dee chee;* seventh)
- ✔ **dì bā** (*dee bah;* eighth)
- ✔ **dì jiǔ** (*dee jyoe;* ninth)
- ✔ **dì shí** (*dee shir;* tenth)

You may need to use these examples to give directions:

- ✔ **dì yī tiáo lù** (*dee ee tyaow loo;* the first street)
- ✔ **dì èr ge fángzi** (*dee are guh fahng dzuh;* the second house)
- ✔ **zuǒ biān dì bā ge fángzi** (*dzwaw byan dee bah guh fahng dzuh;* the eighth house on the left)

If a noun follows the ordinal number, a classifier needs to go in between them, such as **dì bā ge xuéshēng** (*dee bah guh shweh shuhng;* the eighth student) or **dì yī ge háizi** (*dee ee guy hi dzuh;* the first child).

Telling Time

All you have to do to find out the **shíjiān** (*shir jyan;* time) is take a peek at your **shǒubiǎo** (*show byaow;* watch) or look at the **zhōng** (*joong;* clock) on the wall.

You can indicate the hour by saying **3-diǎn** or **3-diǎn zhōng**. **Diǎn** (*dyan*) means "hour," but it's also a classifier, and **zhōng** (*joong*) means "clock." Feel free to use either to say what time it is. (Check out Table 3-3.)

Table 3-3	Telling Time in Chinese	
Chinese Phrase	*Pronunciation*	*English Phrase*
1-diǎn zhōng	ee dyan joong	1 o'clock
2-diǎn zhōng	lyahng dyan joong	2 o'clock
3-diǎn zhōng	sahn dyan joong	3 o'clock
4-diǎn zhōng	suh dyan joong	4 o'clock
5-diǎn zhōng	woo dyan joong	5 o'clock
6-diǎn zhōng	lyo dyan joong	6 o'clock
7-diǎn zhōng	chee dyan joong	7 o'clock
8-diǎn zhōng	bah dyan joong	8 o'clock
9-diǎn zhōng	jyo dyan joong	9 o'clock
10-diǎn zhōng	shir dyan joong	10 o'clock
11-diǎn zhōng	shir ee dyan joong	11 o'clock
12-diǎn zhōng	shir are dyan joong	12 o'clock

When mentioning 12 o'clock, be careful! The way to say noon is simply **zhōngwǔ** (*joong woo*), and the way to say midnight is **bànyè** (*bahn yeh*).

The Chinese are very precise when they tell time. You can't just say **3-diǎn zhōng** (*sahn dyan joong*) when you want to say 3 o'clock; you need to add what part of the day or night you mean:

⮑ **qīngzǎo** (*cheeng dzaow;* midnight to dawn)

⮑ **zǎoshàng** (*dzaow shahng;* 6 a.m. to noon)

⮑ **xiàwǔ** (*shyah woo;* noon to 6 p.m.)

⮑ **wǎnshàng** (*wahn shahng;* 6 p.m. to midnight)

The segment of the day comes before the actual time itself in Chinese:

✔ **wǎnshàng qī diǎn zhōng** (*wahn shahng chee dyan joong;* 7 p.m.)

✔ **xiàwǔ sān diǎn bàn** (*shyah woo sahn dyan bahn;* 3:30 p.m.)

✔ **qīngzǎo yì diǎn yí kè** (*cheeng dzaow ee dyan ee kuh;* 1:15 a.m.)

✔ **zǎoshàng bā diǎn èrshíwǔ fēn** (*dzaow shahng bah dyan are shir woo fun;* 8:25 a.m.)

If you want to indicate half an hour, just add **bàn** (*bahn;* half) after the hour:

✔ **3-diǎn bàn** (*sahn dyan bahn;* 3:30)

✔ **4-diǎn bàn** (*suh dyan bahn;* 4:30)

✔ **11-diǎn bàn** (*shir ee dyan bahn;* 11:30)

Do you want to indicate a quarter of an hour or three quarters of an hour? Just use the phrases **yí kè** (*ee kuh*) and **sān kè** (*sahn kuh*) after the hour:

✔ **2-diǎn yí kè** (*lyahng dyan ee kuh;* 2:15)

✔ **4-diǎn yí kè** (*suh dyan ee kuh;* 4:15)

✔ **5-diǎn sān kè** (*woo dyan sahn kuh;* 5:45)

✔ **7-diǎn sān kè** (*chee dyan sahn kuh;* 7:45)

Here are some other examples of alternative ways to indicate the time:

✔ **chà shí fēn wǔ diǎn** (*chah shir fun woo dyan;* 10 to 5)

✔ **wǔ diǎn chà shí fēn** (*woo dyan chah shir fun;* 10 to 5)

✔ **sì diǎn wǔshí fēn** (*suh dyan woo shir fun;* 4:50)

✔ **chà yí kè qī diǎn** (*chah ee kuh chee dyan;* a quarter to 7)

✔ **qī diǎn chà yí kè** (*chee dyan chah ee kuh;* a quarter to 7)

✔ **liù diǎn sān kè** (*lyo dyan sahn kuh;* 6:45)

✔ **liù diǎn sìshíwǔ fēn** (*lyo dyan suh shir woo fun;* 6:45)

When talking about time, you may prefer to say
before or after a certain hour. To do so, you use either
yǐqián (*ee chyan;* before) or **yǐhòu** (*ee ho;* after). Here
are some examples:

✔ **xiàwǔ 3-diǎn zhōng yǐqián** (*shyah woo sahn
dyan joong ee chyan;* before 3:00 p.m.)

✔ **qīngzǎo 5-diǎn bàn yǐhòu** (*cheeng dzaow woo
dyan bahn ee ho;* after 5:30 a.m.)

Monday, Tuesday: Weekdays

Although Chinese people recognize seven days in the
week just as Americans do, the Chinese week begins
on **xīngqīyī** (*sheeng chee ee;* Monday) and ends on
xīngqītiān (*sheeng chee tyan;* Sunday). See Table 3-4
for a list of days of the week.

Table 3-4	Days of the Week	
Chinese Word	*Pronunciation*	*English Word*
xīngqīyī	sheeng chee ee	Monday
xīngqī'èr	sheeng chee are	Tuesday
xīngqīsān	sheeng chee sahn	Wednesday
xīngqīsì	sheeng chee suh	Thursday
xīngqīwǔ	sheeng chee woo	Friday
xīngqīliù	sheeng chee lyo	Saturday
xīngqītiān	sheeng chee tyan	Sunday

So, **jīntiān xīngqījǐ?** (*jin tyan sheeng chee jee;* What
day is it today?) Where does today fit in your weekly
routine?

✔ **Jīntiān xīngqī'èr.** (*jin tyan sheeng chee are;* Today is Tuesday.)

✔ **Wǒ xīngqīyī dào xīngqīwǔ gōngzuò.** (*waw sheeng chee ee daow sheeng chee woo goong dzwaw;* I work from Monday to Friday.)

✔ **Wǒmen měige xīngqīyī kāihuì.** (*waw mun may guh sheeng chee ee kye hway;* We have meetings every Monday.)

✔ **Xiàge xīngqīsān shì wǒde shēngrì.** (*shyah guh sheeng chee sahn shir waw duh shung ir;* Next Wednesday is my birthday.)

Words to Know

houtiān	ho tyan	the day after tomorrow
jīntiān	jin tyan	today
míngtiān	meeng tyan	tomorrow
qiántiān	chyan tyan	the day before yesterday
shàngge xīngqī	shahng guh sheeng chee	last week
xiàge xīngqī	shyah guh sheeng chee	next week
zhèige xīngqī	jay guh sheeng sheeng chee	this week
zuótiān	dzwaw tyan	yesterday

Using the Calendar and Dates

To ask what today's date is, you simply say **Jīntiān jǐyuè jǐhào?** (*jin tyan jee yweh jee how; literally:* Today is what month and what day?)

When answering, remember that the larger unit of the month always comes before the smaller unit of the date in Chinese:

> ✔ **Yīyuè èr hào** (*ee yweh are how;* January 2nd)
>
> ✔ **Sānyuè sì hào** (*sahn yweh suh how;* March 4th)
>
> ✔ **Shí'èryuè sānshí hào** (*shir are yweh sahn shir how;* December 30th)

I list the months of the year in Table 3-5 and the seasons in Table 3-6.

Table 3-5	Months of the Year and Other Pertinent Terms	
Chinese Word or Phrase	*Pronunciation*	*English Word or Phrase*
yīyuè	ee yweh	January
èryuè	are yweh	February
sānyuè	sahn yweh	March
sìyuè	suh yweh	April
wǔyuè	woo yweh	May
liùyuè	lyo yweh	June
qīyuè	chee yweh	July
bāyuè	bah yweh	August
jiǔyuè	jyo yweh	September
shíyuè	shir yweh	October
shíyīyuè	shir ee yweh	November

Chinese Word or Phrase	Pronunciation	English Word or Phrase
shí'èryuè	shir are yweh	December
zhèige yuè	jay guh yweh	this month
shàngge yuè	shahng guh yweh	last month
xiàge yuè	shyah guh yweh	next month
shēngrì	shung er	birthday

Table 3-6	Seasonal Terms	
Chinese Word or Phrase	Pronunciation	English Word or Phrase
sì jì	suh jee	The four seasons
dōngjì	doong jee	winter
chūnjì	chwun jee	spring
xiàjì	shyah jee	summer
qiūjì	chyo jee	fall

Even though you say each month by adding the number of the month in front of the word **yuè** (which means "month"), if you add the classifier **ge** (*guh*) in between the number and the word **yuè**, you say "one month," "two months," and so on. For example, **bā yuè** (*bah yweh*) means August (which is the 8th month), but **bā ge yuè** (*bah guh yweh*) means eight months.

You can't check out the months of the year without first looking at the holidays. First you celebrate

✔ **Xīnnián** (*shin nyan;* New Year's Day; also known as **yuándàn**; *ywan dahn*) on **yī yuè yī hào** (*ee yweh ee how;* January 1st).

✔ **Chūn jié** (*chwun jyeh;* Spring Festival, or Chinese New Year). This a three-day celebration coinciding with the lunar new year. Every year the dates for **chūn jié** change because it follows the **yīnlì** (*yeen lee;* lunar calendar) rather than the **yánglì** (*yahng lee;* solar calendar). **Chūn jié** always occurs sometime in January or February.

If you travel to China **jīn nián** (*jin nyan;* this year) during 2005, you arrive during **jī nián** (*jee nyan;* the Year of the Rooster). Want to travel in the coming years instead?

✔ 2006: **gǒu nián** (*go nyan*); Year of the Dog

✔ 2007: **zhū nián** (*joo nyan*); Year of the Pig

✔ 2008: **shǔ nián** (*shoo nyan*); Year of the Rat

The Year of the Rat is actually the beginning of a whole new 12-year cycle of animals. Table 3-7 shows all the animals of the Chinese zodiac. Just as in Western astrology, each of the Chinese animals represents a different personality type.

Table 3-7	Animals of the Chinese Zodiac	
Chinese Word	*Pronunciation*	*English Word*
shǔ	shoo	rat
niú	nyo	ox
hǔ	hoo	tiger
tùzi	too dzuh	rabbit
lóng	loong	dragon
shé	shuh	snake

Chinese Word	Pronunciation	English Word
mǎ	mah	horse
yáng	yahng	goat
hóu	ho	monkey
jī	jee	rooster
gǒu	go	dog
zhū	joo	pig

In mainland China, **Láodòng jié** (*laow doong jyeh;* Labor Day) is celebrated on **wǔ yuè yī hào** (*woo yweh ee how;* May 1st), and **Guó qìng jié** (*gwaw cheeng jyeh;* National Day) is celebrated on **shí yuè yī hào** (*shir yweh ee how;* October 1st) in commemoration of the day Mao Zedong and the Chinese Communist Party declared the founding of the **Zhōnghuá rénmín gònghé guó** (*joong hwah run meen goong huh gwaw;* the People's Republic of China) in 1949. In Taiwan, **Guó qìng jié** is celebrated on **shí yuè shí hào** (*shir yweh shir how;* October 10th) to commemorate the day in 1911 when China's long dynastic history ended and a new era of the **Zhōnghuá mín guó** (*joong hwah meen gwaw;* the Republic of China) began, under the leadership of Dr. Sun Yat-sen.

In Taiwan, you often see years written out that seem to be 11 years short of what you think is correct. That's because the founding of the Republic of China in 1911 is considered the base line for all future years. So 1921 is listed as **mín guó shí nián** (*meen gwaw shir nyan;* "meen gwaw" is the abbreviation for **Zhōnghuá mín guó** [*joong hwah meen gwaw*], or the Republic of China, and "shir nyan," meaning 10 years, refers to 10 years following the founding of the Republic of China). The year 2005 is noted as **mín guó jiǔshí sì nián** (*meen gwaw jyo shir suh nyan;* 94 years after the establishment of the Republic of China).

Words to Know

hòunián	ho nyan	the year after next
jīnnián	jin nyan	this year
měinián	may nyan	every year
míngnián	meeng nyan	next year
shàngge xīngqīsì	shahng guh sheeng chee suh	last Thursday
qiánnián	chyan nyan	the year before last
qùnián	chyew nyan	last year
xiàge xīngqīyī	shyah guh sheeng chee ee	next Monday
Zhù nǐ shēngrì kuàilè!	joo nee shung ir kwye luh	Happy Birthday!

Money, Money, Money

Qián (*chyan;* money) makes the world go around. In this section, pick up important words and phrases for acquiring and spending money.

The basic elements of all Chinese currency are the **yuán** (colloquially referred to as a **kuài**), which you can think of as a dollar, the **jiǎo** (colloquially referred to as the **máo**), which is the equivalent of a dime, and the **fēn** (*fun*), which is equivalent to the penny.

Want to know how much money I have right now in my pocket, Nosy? Why not just ask me?

✔ **Nǐ yǒu jǐ kuài qián?** (*nee yo jee kwye chyan;* How much money do you have?)

Use this phrase if you assume the amount is less than $10.

✔ **Nǐ yǒu duōshǎo qián?** (*nee yo dwaw shaow chyan;* How much money do you have?)

Use this phrase if you assume the amount is greater than $10.

Making and exchanging money

You can always **huàn qián** (*hwahn chyan;* exchange money) the minute you arrive at the **fēijī chǎng** (*fay jee chahng;* airport) at the many **duìhuànchù** (*dway hwahn choo;* exchange bureaus), or you can wait until you get to a major **yínháng** (*een hahng;* bank) or check in at your **lǚguǎn** (*lyew gwahn;* hotel).

The following phrases come in handy when you're ready to **huàn qián:**

✔ **Qǐng wèn, zài nǎr kěyǐ huàn qián?** (*cheeng one, dzye nar kuh yee hwahn chyan;* Excuse me, where can I change money?)

✔ **Qǐng wèn, yínháng zài nǎr?** (*cheeng one, eeng hahng dzye nar;* Excuse me, where is the bank?)

✔ **Jīntiān de duìhuàn lǜ shì shénme?** (*jin tyan duh dway hwahn lyew shir shummuh;* What's today's exchange rate?)

✔ **Qǐng nǐ gěi wǒ sì zhāng wǔshí yuán de.** (*cheeng nee gay waw suh jahng woo shir ywan duh;* Please give me four 50-yuan bills.)

✔ **Wǒ yào huàn yì bǎi měiyuán.** (*waw yaow hwahn ee bye may ywan;* I'd like to change $100.)

✔ **Nǐmen shōu duōshǎo qián shǒuxùfèi?** (*nee mun show dwaw shaow chyan show shyew fay;* How much commission do you charge?)

Words to Know

chūnàyuán	choo nah ywan	cashier
duìhuàn lǜ	dway hwahn lyew	exchange rate
duìhuànchù	dway hwahn choo	exchange counter
huàn	hwahn	to exchange
huàn qián	hwahn chyan	to exchange money
měiyuán	may ywan	U.S. dollars
Qǐng gěi wǒ kànkàn nǐde hùzhào.	Cheeng gay waw kahn kahn nee duh hoo jaow.	Please show me your passport.
rénmínbì	run meen bee	Chinese dollar (mainland)
shǒuxùfèi	show shyew fay	commission
wàibì	why bee	foreign currency
xīn táibì	shin tye bee	New Taiwan dollars
yì měiyuán	ee may ywan	one U.S. dollar

Cashing checks and checking your cash

When you talk about how much something costs, you put the numerical value before the word for bill or coin. For example, you can call a dollar **yí kuài** (*ee kwye;* one dollar) or **sān kuài** (*sahn kwye;* three dollars). You translate 10 cents, literally, as one 10-cent coin — **yì máo** (*ee maow*) — or 30 cents as, literally, three 10-cent coins — **sān máo** (*sahn maow*).

Here's how you speak of increasing amounts of money. You mention the larger units before the smaller units, just like in English:

- ✔ **sān kuài** (*sahn kwye;* $3)

- ✔ **sān kuài yì máo** (*sahn kwye ee maow;* $3.10)

- ✔ **sān kuài yì máo wǔ** (*sahn kwye ee maow woo;* $3.15)

- ✔ **Qǐng wèn, zhè jiàn yīfu duōshǎo qián?** (*Cheeng one, jay jyan ee foo dwaw shaow chyan;* Excuse me, how much is this piece of clothing?)

- ✔ **Nǐmen shōu bù shōu zhīpiào?** (*nee mun show boo show jir pyaow;* Do you take checks?)

- ✔ **Nǐmen shōu bù shōu xìnyòng kǎ?** (*nee mun show boo show sheen yoong kah;* Do you accept credit cards?)

Words to Know

dà piàozi	dah pyaow dzuh	large bills
fù zhàng	foo jahng	to pay a bill
		continued

Words to Know *(continued)*

huàn kāi	hwahn kye	to break (a large bill)
kǒudài	ko dye	pocket
língqián	leeng chyan	small change
lǚxíng zhīpiào	lyew sheeng jir pyaow	traveler's checks
qiánbāo	chyan baow	wallet; purse
zhīpiào	jir pyaow	checks
zhīpiào bù	jir pyaow boo	checkbook

Doing your banking

If you plan on staying in Asia for an extended time or you want to continue doing business with a Chinese company, you may want to open a **huóqī zhànghù** (*hwaw chee jahng hoo;* checking account) where you can both **cún qián** (*tswun chyan;* deposit money) and **qǔ qián** (*chyew chyan;* withdraw money). If you stay long enough, consider opening a **dìngqī cúnkuǎn hùtóu** (*deeng chee tswun kwan hoo toe;* savings account) so you can start earning some **lìxi** (*lee she;* interest). Earning interest sure beats stuffing **dà piàozi** (*dah pyaow dzuh;* large bills) under your **chuáng diàn** (*chwahng dyan;* mattress) for years.

How about trying to make your money work for you by investing in one of the following:

- ✔ **chǔxù cúnkuǎn** (*chew shyew tswun kwan;* Certificate of Deposit; CD)
- ✔ **guókù quàn** (*gwaw koo chwan;* treasury bond)

> ✔ **gǔpiào** (*goo pyaow;* stock)
>
> ✔ **hùzhù jījīn** (*hoo joo jee jeen;* mutual fund)
>
> ✔ **tàotóu jījīn** (*taow toe jee jeen;* hedge fund)
>
> ✔ **zhàiquàn** (*jye chwan;* bond)

If you plan to cash some checks along with your deposits, here are a couple useful phrases to know:

> ✔ **Wǒ yào duìxiàn zhèi zhāng zhīpiào.** (*waw yaow dway shyan jay jahng jir pyaow;* I'd like to cash this check.)
>
> ✔ **Bèimiàn qiān zì xiě zài nǎr?** (*bay myan chyan dzuh shyeh dzye nar;* Where shall I endorse it?)

Words to Know

chūnà chuāngkǒu	choo nah chwahng ko	cashier's window
chūnàyuán	choo nah ywan	bank teller
cúnkuǎn	tswun kwan	savings
cún qián	tswun chyan	to deposit money
kāi yíge cúnkuǎn hùtóu	kye ee guh tswun kwan hoo toe	to open a savings account
qǔ qián	chyew chyan	to withdraw money
yínháng	eeng hahng	bank
xiànjīn	shyan jeen	cash

Accessing an ATM machine

Zìdòng tíkuǎnjī (*dzuh doong tee kwan jee;* ATM machines) are truly ubiquitous these days. In order to use one, you need a **zìdòng tíkuǎn kǎ** (*dzuh doong tee kwan kah;* ATM card) to find out your **jiéyú** (*jyeh yew;* account balance), to **cún qián** (*tswun chyan;* deposit money), or to **qǔ qián** (*chyew chyan;* withdraw money). And you definitely need to know your **mìmǎ** (*mee mah;* PIN number); otherwise, the **zìdòng tíkuǎnjī** is useless.

And one more thing: Make sure you don't let anyone else know your **mìmǎ**. It's your **mìmì** (*mee mee;* secret).

Words to Know		
tóngyì	toong ee	to agree
yígòng	ee goong	altogether
yīnggāi	eeng guy	should
yīnwèi . . . suǒyǐ	een way . . . swaw yee	because . . . therefore
zhàngdān	jahng dahn	bill

Chapter 4

Making New Friends and Enjoying Small Talk

● ●

In This Chapter

▶ Introducing yourself and others

▶ Using question words

▶ Greeting and chatting with family, friends, and colleagues

● ●

*N*ǐ hǎo! (*nee how;* Hello!; How are you?) These two words are probably the most important you need to know to start a conversation.

In this chapter, I show you how to greet people, introduce yourself, and make small talk.

Making Introductions

Nothing beats making new friends at a **wǎnhuì** (*wahn hway;* party), a **xīn gōngzuò** (*sheen goong dzwaw;* new job), on the **dìtiě** (*dee tyeh;* subway), or just **zài lùshàng** (*dzye loo shahng;* on the street). This section gives you a head start in making a good first impression.

Acquainting yourself

You have options other than **nǐ hǎo** (*nee how;* hi; how are you) when you first meet someone, such as

> ✔ **Hěn gāoxìng jiàndào nǐ.** (*hun gaow sheeng jyan daow nee;* Glad to meet you.)
>
> ✔ **Wǒ hěn róngxìng.** (*waw hun roong sheeng;* I'm honored to meet you.)

Or if you want a time-specific greeting, try

> ✔ **zǎo** (*dzaow;* good morning)
>
> ✔ **zǎo ān** (*dzaow ahn;* good morning; *literally:* early peace)
>
> ✔ **wǎn ān** (*wahn ahn;* good night)

Don't know what to say after the first **nǐ hǎo?** The following are a few examples of common opening lines to get you started:

> ✔ **Qǐng ràng wǒ jièshào wǒ zìjǐ.** (*cheeng rahng waw jyeh shaow waw dzuh jee;* Please let me introduce myself.)
>
> ✔ **Wǒ jiào _____. Nǐ ne?** (*waw jyaow _____. nee nuh;* My name is _____. What's yours?)
>
> ✔ **Nǐ jiào shénme míngzi?** (*nee jyaow shummuh meeng dzuh;* What's your name?)
>
> ✔ **Wǒ shì Měiguórén.** (*waw shir may gwaw run;* I'm an American.)

Introducing your friends and family

To introduce your friends to each other, say "**Qǐng ràng wǒ jièshào wǒde péngyǒu, Carl.**" (*cheeng rahng waw jyeh shaow waw duh puhng yo, Carl;* May I please introduce my friend, Carl.) In addition to introducing your **péngyǒu** (*puhng yo;* friend), you can also introduce these important people:

- ✔ **àirén** (*eye run;* spouse — used mostly in mainland China [as opposed to Taiwan])
- ✔ **bàba** (*bah bah;* father)
- ✔ **érzi** (*are dzuh;* son)
- ✔ **fùmǔ** (*foo moo;* parents)
- ✔ **mǔqin** (*moo cheen;* mother)
- ✔ **fùqin** (*foo cheen;* father)
- ✔ **háizi** (*hi dzuh;* children)
- ✔ **lǎobǎn** (*laow bahn;* boss)
- ✔ **lǎoshī** (*laow shir;* teacher)
- ✔ **māma** (*mah mah;* mother)
- ✔ **nán péngyǒu** (*nahn puhng yo;* boyfriend)
- ✔ **nǚ'ér** (*nyew are;* daughter)
- ✔ **nǚpéngyǒu** (*nyew pung yo;* girlfriend)
- ✔ **qīzi** (*chee dzuh;* wife)
- ✔ **sūnnǚ** (*swun nyew;* granddaughter)
- ✔ **sūnzi** (*swun dzuh;* grandson)
- ✔ **tàitài** (*tye tye;* wife — used mostly in Taiwan)
- ✔ **tóngshì** (*toong shir;* colleague)
- ✔ **tóngwū** (*toong woo;* roommate)
- ✔ **tóngxué** (*toong shweh;* classmate)
- ✔ **wǒde péngyǒu** (*waw duh puhng yo;* my friend)
- ✔ **xiōngdì jiěmèi** (*shyoong dee jyeh may;* brothers and sisters)
- ✔ **zhàngfu** (*jahng foo;* husband)
- ✔ **zǔfù** (*dzoo foo;* grandfather)
- ✔ **zǔmǔ** (*dzoo moo;* grandmother)

When introducing two people to each other, always introduce the one with the lower social status and/or age to the person with the higher social status. The Chinese consider it polite.

Asking people for their names

Many situations call for informal greetings like

> ✔ **Wǒ jiào Sarah. Nǐ ne?** (*waw jyaow Sarah. nee nuh;* My name is Sarah. And yours?)
>
> ✔ **Nǐ jiào shénme míngzi?** (*nee jyaow shummuh meeng dzuh;* What's your name?)

To show a greater level of politeness and respect, ask

Nín guì xìng? (*neen gway sheeng; literally:* What's your honorable surname?)

When answering this question, don't use the honorific **guì** to refer to yourself. Such a response is like saying "My esteemed family name is Smith." The best way to answer is to say **Wǒ xìng Smith.** (*waw sheeng Smith;* My family name is Smith.)

The polite way to ask the name of someone who's younger than yourself or lower in social status is

Nǐ jiào shénme míngzi? (*nee jyaow shummuh meeng dzuh;* What's your name?)

Even though **míngzi** usually means *"given name,"* when you ask this question, it may elicit an answer of first and last name.

If a guy tells you his name in Chinese, you can be sure the first syllable he utters will be his surname, not his given name. So if he says his name is **Lǐ Shìmín,** for example, his family name is **Lǐ** and his given name is **Shìmín.** Keep on referring to him as **Lǐ Shìmín** (rather than just **Shìmín**) until you become really good friends. If you want to address him as **Xiānshēng** (*shyan shuhng;* Mr.), or if you're addressing a female as **Xiǎojiě** (*shyaow jyeh;* Miss), you put that title after his or her last name and say **Lǐ Xiānshēng** or **Lǐ Xiǎojiě.** Even though the Chinese language has words for Mr., Miss, and Mrs. (**tàitài;** *tye tye*), it doesn't have an equivalent term for "Ms." At least not yet.

This little conversation shows how to introduce a friend:

Sylvia: **Irene, qǐng ràng wǒ jièshào wǒde péngyǒu Mel.** (*Irene, cheeng rahng waw jyeh shaow waw duh puhng yo Mel;* Irene, allow me to introduce my friend Mel.)

Irene: **Nǐ hǎo. Hěn gāoxìng jiàndào nǐ.** (*nee how. hun gaow sheeng jyan daow nee;* Hi. Nice to meet you.)

Mel: **Hěn gāoxìng jiàndào nǐ. Wǒ shì Sylvia de tóngxué.** (*hun gaow sheeng jyan daow nee. waw shir Sylvia duh toong shweh;* Good to meet you. I'm Sylvia's classmate.)

Irene: **Hěn gāoxìng jiàndào nǐ.** (*hun gaow sheeng jyan daow nee;* Nice to meet you.)

Mel: **Nǐmen zénme rènshì?** (*nee mun dzummuh run shir;* How do you happen to know each other?)

Irene: **Wǒmen shì tóngshì.** (*waw mun shir toong shir;* We're coworkers.)

Addressing new friends and strangers

You can always safely greet people in professional settings by announcing their last name followed by their title, such as **Wáng Xiàozhǎng** (*wahng shyaow jahng;* President [of an educational institution] Wang) or **Jīn Zhǔrèn** (*jeen joo run;* Director Jin). Here are some other examples of occupational titles:

- ✔ **bùzhǎng** (*boo jahng;* department head or minister)

- ✔ **fùzhǔrèn** (*foo joo run;* assistant director)

- ✔ **jiàoshòu** (*jyaow show;* professor)

- ✔ **jīnglǐ** (*jeeng lee;* manager)

- ✔ **lǎoshī** (*laow shir;* teacher)

Sometimes people add the terms **lǎo** (*laow;* old) or **xiǎo** (*shyaow;* young) in front of the last name and omit the first name completely. It indicates a comfortable degree of familiarity and friendliness that can only develop over time. But make sure you know which one to use — **lǎo** is for someone who's older than you, and **xiǎo** is for someone who's younger than you.

Taking (a.k.a. rejecting) compliments

Chinese people are always impressed whenever they meet a foreigner who has taken the time to learn their language. So when you speak **Zhōngwén** (*joong one;* Chinese) to a **Zhōngguórén** (*joong gwaw run;* Chinese person), he may very well say **"Nǐde Zhōngwén tài hǎole."** (*nee duh joong one tye how luh;* Your Chinese is fantastic.) But don't give in to the temptation to accept the compliment easily and say **xièxiè** (*shyeh shyeh;* thanks), because that implies that you agree wholeheartedly with the complimentary assessment. Instead, try one of the following replies. Each of them can be roughly translated as "It's nothing" or the equivalent of "No, no, I don't deserve any praise."

- ✔ **guò jiǎng guò jiǎng** (*gwaw jyahng gwaw jyahng*)
- ✔ **nálǐ nálǐ** (*nah lee nah lee*)
- ✔ **nǎr de huà** (*nar duh hwah*)

Saying goodbye

When it comes time to say goodbye, refer to the following list of phrases:

- ✔ **Huítóu jiàn.** (*hway toe jyan;* See you later.)
- ✔ **Míngnián jiàn.** (*meeng nyan jyan;* See you next year.)
- ✔ **Míngtiān jiàn.** (*meeng tyan jyan;* See you tomorrow.)

✔ **Xiàge lǐbài jiàn.** (*shyah guh lee bye jyan;* See you next week.)

✔ **Xīngqī'èr jiàn.** (*sheeng chee are jyan;* See you on Tuesday.)

✔ **Yīhuǐr jiàn.** (*ee hwahr jyan;* See you soon.)

✔ **Yílù píng'ān.** (*ee loo peeng ahn;* Have a good trip.)

✔ **Zài jiàn.** (*dzye jyan;* Goodbye.)

Practice your adieu's with this conversation:

Christopher: **Lǎoshī zǎo.** (*laow shir dzaow;* Good morning, Professor.)

Professor: **Zǎo. Nǐ hǎo.** (*dzaow. nee how;* Good morning. Hello.)

Christopher: **Jīntiān de tiānqì hěn hǎo, duì búduì?** (*jin tyan duh tyan chee hun how, dway boo dway;* The weather today is great, isn't it?)

Professor: **Duìle. Hěn hǎo.** (*dway luh. hun how;* Yes, it is. It's very nice.)

Christopher: **Nèmme míngtiān shàngkè de shíhòu zài jiàn.** (*nummuh, meeng tyan shahng kuh duh shir ho dzye jyan;* So, I'll see you again in class tomorrow.)

Professor: **Hǎo. Míngtiān jiàn.** (*how. meeng tyan jyan;* Okay. See you tomorrow.)

Asking Basic Questions

A surefire way of initiating a conversation is to ask someone a question. Here are some basic question words to keep in mind:

✔ **Duō jiǔ?** (*dwaw jyoe;* For how long?)

✔ **Shéi** (*shay;* Who?)

✔ **Shénme?** (*shummuh;* What?)

✔ **Shénme shíhòu?** (*shummuh shir ho;* When?)

✔ **Wèishénme?** (*way shummuh;* Why?)

✔ **Zài nǎr?** (*dzye nar;* Where?)

✔ **Zěnme?** (*dzummah;* How?)

These examples can help you use these question words in simple sentences — sometimes you can also use some of them on their own, just as in English:

✔ **Tā shì shéi?** (*tah shir shay;* Who is he/she?)

✔ **Nǐ yào shénme?** (*nee yaow shummuh;* What would you like?)

✔ **Jǐ diǎn zhōng?** (*jee dyan joong;* What time is it?)

✔ **Cèsuǒ zài nǎr?** (*tsuh swaw dzye nar;* Where's the bathroom?)

✔ **Nǐ shénme shíhòu chīfàn?** (*nee shummuh shir ho chir fahn;* When do you eat?)

✔ **Nǐ wèishénme yào qù Zhōngguó?** (*nee way shummuh yaow chyew joong gwaw;* Why do you want to go to China?)

✔ **Nǐ zěnme yàng?** (*nee dzummah yahng;* How's it going?)

✔ **Nǐ yǐjīng zài zhèr duō jiǔ le?** (*nee ee jeeng dzye jar dwaw jyoe luh;* How long have you been here already?)

✔ **Xiànzài jǐ diǎn zhōng?** (*shyan dzye jee dyan joong;* What time is it now?)

You can also use the following responses to the questions in the preceding list if someone happens to approach you. These statements are the basics of small talk and really come in handy when studying a foreign language:

✔ **Wǒ bùdǒng.** (*waw boo doong;* I don't understand.)

✔ **Wǒ bùzhīdào.** (*waw boo jir daow;* I don't know.)

✔ **Wǒ búrènshi tā.** (*waw boo run shir tah;* I don't know him/her.)

▰ **Duìbùqǐ.** (*dway boo chee;* Excuse me.)

▰ **Hěn bàoqiàn.** (*hun baow chyan;* I'm so sorry.)

The following dialog incorporates some basic questions:

Molly: **Duìbùqǐ. Qǐngwèn, xiànzài jǐdiǎn zhōng?** (*dway boo chee. cheeng one, shyan dzye jee dyan joong;* Excuse me. May I ask what time is it?)

Man: **Xiànzài yīdiǎn bàn.** (*shyan dzye ee dyan bahn;* It's 1:30.)

Molly: **Hǎo. Xièxiè nǐ.** (*how. shyeh shyeh nee;* Great. Thank you.)

Man: **Bú kèqì.** (*boo kuh chee;* You're welcome.)

Molly: **Máfán nǐ, sì lù chēzhàn zài nǎr?** (*mah fahn nee, suh loo chuh jahn dzye nar;* Sorry to trouble you again, but where's the No. 4 bus stop?)

Man: **Chēzhàn jiù zài nàr.** (*chuh jahn jyoe dzye nar;* The bus stop is just over there.)

Molly: **Hǎo. Xièxiè.** (*how. shyeh shyeh;* Okay. Thanks.)

Man: **Méi wèntí.** (*may one tee;* No problem.)

Words to Know

chēzhàn	chuh jahn	bus stop
méi wèntí	may one tee	no problem
Xiànzài jǐ diǎn zhōng?	shyan dzye jee dyan joong	What time is it?

The following is a list of simple questions you can use when you meet people.

✔ **Nǐ jiào shénme míngzi?** (*nee jyaow shummuh meeng dzuh;* What's your name?)

✔ **Nǐ niánjì duō dà?** (*nee nyan jee dwaw dah;* How old are you?)

✔ **Nǐ zhù zài nǎr?** (*nee joo dzye nar;* Where do you live?)

✔ **Nǐ jiéhūn le méiyǒu?** (*nee jyeh hwun luh mayo;* Are you married?)

✔ **Nǐ yǒu háizi ma?** (*nee yo hi dzuh mah;* Do you have children?)

✔ **Nǐ zuò shénme gōngzuò?** (*nee dzwaw shummuh goong dzwaw;* What kind of work do you do?)

✔ **Nǐ huì jiǎng Zhōngwén ma?** (*nee hway jyahng joong one mah;* Do you speak Chinese?)

✔ **Nǐ xǐhuān kàn diànyǐng ma?** (*nee she hwahn kahn dyan yeeng mah;* Do you like to see movies?)

✔ **Nǐ shénme shíhòu zǒu?** (*nee shummuh shir ho dzoe;* When are you leaving?)

✔ **Jīntiān de tiānqì zěnme yàng?** (*jin tyan duh tyan chee dzummah yahng;* How's the weather today?)

Chatting It Up

Xiánliáo (*shyan lyaow*) means "small talk" in Chinese. **Xiántán** (*shyan tahn*) is "to chat" . . . either term does the trick. This section helps you master a few key phrases and questions you can use to establish a relationship.

Yakking about the weather

Talking about the **tiānqì** (*tyan chee;* weather) is always a safe topic in any conversation. In fact, it's kind of the universal icebreaker. If the skies are blue and all seems right with the world, you can start by saying

Jīntiān de tiānqì zhēn hǎo, duì bú duì? (*jin tyan duh tyan chee juhn how, dway boo dway;* The weather today is sure nice, isn't it?)

The following adjectives can help you describe temperature and humidity:

- **lěng** (*lung;* cold)
- **liángkuài** (*lyahng kwye;* cool)
- **mēnrè** (*mun ruh;* muggy)
- **nuǎnhuó** (*nwan hwaw;* warm)
- **rè** (*ruh;* hot)

The **sìjì** (*suh jee;* four seasons) — **dōngtiān** (*doong tyan;* winter), **chūntiān** (*chwun tyan;* spring), **xiàtiān** (*shyah tyan;* summer), and **qiūtiān** (*chyo tyan;* fall) — all have their charms. They also all have their distinctive characteristics when it comes to the weather, which you can express with the following words in any conversation:

- **bàofēngxuě** (*baow fuhng shweh;* blizzard)
- **dàfēng** (*dah fuhng;* gusty winds)
- **duōyún** (*dwaw yewn;* cloudy)
- **fēng hěn dà** (*fuhng hun dah;* windy)
- **léiyǔ** (*lay yew;* thunderstorm)
- **qínglǎng** (*cheeng lahng;* sunny)
- **qíngtiān** (*cheeng tyan;* clear)
- **xià máomáoyǔ** (*shyah maow maow yew;* drizzle)
- **xiàwù** (*shyah woo;* fog)
- **xiàxuě** (*shyah shweh;* snow)
- **xiàyǔ** (*shyah yew;* rainy)
- **yīntiān** (*yeen tyan;* overcast)

Try out this small talk on the weather:

Jean: **Hā'ěrbīn dōngtiān hěn lěng. Chángcháng xiàxuě.** (*hah are been doong tyan hun lung. chahng chahng shyah shweh;* Harbin is very cold in the winter. It snows often.*)

Bill: **Zhēnde ma?** (*jun duh mah;* Really?)

Jean: **Zhēnde. Yě yǒu bàofēngxuě. Xiàtiān hái hǎo. Bǐjiào nuǎnhuó.** (*jun duh. yeh yo baow fuhng shweh. shyah tyan hi how. bee jyaow nwan hwaw;* Really. There are also blizzards. Summertime is okay, though. It's relatively warm.)

Bill: **Lěng tiān kéyǐ qù huáxuě, hái kéyǐ qù liūbīng. Nèmme Hā'ěrbīn dōngtiān de shíhòu hěn hǎo wán.** (*lung tyan kuh yee chyew hwah shweh, hi kuh yee chyew lyo beeng. nummah hah are been doong tyan duh shir ho hun how wahn;* In cold weather, you can go skiing or ice-skating. So Harbin during the winter is a lot of fun.)

Finding out where people are from

Wondering where people are from when you first meet them is only natural. You ask them by saying

> **Nǐ shì cóng nǎr láide?** (*nee shir tsoong nar lye duh;* Where are you from?)

To answer, you replace the word **nǐ** (*nee;* you) with **wǒ** (*waw;* I) and put the name of wherever you're from where the word **nǎr** is.

> **Wǒ shì cóng Paris láide.** (*waw shir tsoong paris lye duh;* I am from Paris.)

 People in Taiwan say **nálǐ** (*nah lee*) rather than **nǎr** (*nar*) for the word "where." **Nǎr** indicates a northern accent and is used primarily by people from mainland China.

This list includes countries that may come up in conversation:

✔ **Àudàlìyà** (*ow dah lee yah;* Australia)

✔ **Fǎguó** (*fah gwaw;* France)

✔ **Měiguó** (*may gwaw;* America)

✔ **Rìběn** (*ir bun;* Japan)

✔ **Ruìdiǎn** (*rway dyan;* Sweden)

✔ **Ruìshì** (*rway shir;* Switzerland)

✔ **Yìdàlì** (*ee dah lee;* Italy)

✔ **Yīngguó** (*eeng gwaw;* England)

✔ **Yuènán** (*yweh nahn;* Vietnam)

✔ **Zhōngguó** (*joong gwaw;* China)

A little chat about where you're from:

Cynthia: **Adrienne, nǐ shì cóng nǎr láide?**
(*Adrienne, nee shir tsoong nar lye duh;* Adrienne, where are you from?)

Adrienne: **Wǒ shì cóng Jiāzhōu láide. Nǐ ne?**
(*waw shir tsoong jyah joe lye duh. nee nuh;* I'm from California. How about you?)

Cynthia: **Wǒ búshì Měiguórén. Wǒ shì cóng Yīngguó Lúndūn láide.** (*waw boo shir may gwaw run. waw shir tsoong eeng gwaw lwun dun lye duh;* I'm not American. I'm from London, England.)

Adrienne: **Nà tài hǎole.** (*nah tye how luh;* That's great.)

Words to Know

Jiāzhōu	jyah joe	California
Měiguórén	may gwaw run	American
Nà tài hǎole	nah tye how luh	That's great.
Yīngguó	eeng gwaw	England

Chatting about family

If you want to talk about your family when answering questions or making small talk, you need to know who is in your family. (Check out "Introducing your friends and family" earlier in this chapter for important vocabulary words.)

Join with these women chatting about their families:

Lǐ Huá: **Beverly, nǐ yǒu méiyǒu xiōngdì jiěmèi?** (*Beverly, nee yo mayo shyoong dee jyeh may;* Beverly, do you have any brothers or sisters?)

Beverly: **Wǒ yǒu yíge jiějie. Tā shíwǔ suì. Bǐ wǒ dà liǎngsuì.** (*waw yo ee guh jyeh jyeh. tah shir woo sway. bee waw dah lyahng sway;* I have an older sister. She's 15. She's two years older than me.)

Lǐ Huá: **Tā yě huì jiǎng Zhōngwén ma?** (*tah yeah hway jyahng joong one mah;* Can she also speak Chinese?)

Beverly: **Búhuì. Tā zhǐ huì Yīngyǔ.** (*boo hway. tah jir hway eeng yew;* No. She only speaks English.)

Lǐ Huá: **Nǐde fùmǔ zhù zài nǎr?** (*nee duh foo moo joo dzye nar;* Where do your parents live?)

Beverly: **Wǒmen dōu zhù zài Běijīng. Wǒ bàba shì wàijiāoguān.** (*waw men doe joo dzye bay jeeng. waw bah bah shir why jyaow gwan;* We all live in Beijing. My father is a diplomat.)

Words to Know

jiǎng	jyahng	to talk
wàijiāoguān	why jyaow gwahn	diplomat
Yīngyǔ	eeng yew	English

Zhōngwén	joong one	Chinese
zhù	joo	to live

Making small talk on the job

The kind of job you have can say plenty about you. It can also be a great topic of conversation or spice up an otherwise dull exchange. To ask someone about his or her **gōngzuò** (*goong dzwaw;* work), you can say

> **Nǐ zuò shénme gōngzuò?** (*nee dzwaw shummuh goong dzwaw;* What kind of work do you do?)

You may even try to guess and say, for example,

> **Nǐ shì lǎoshī ma?** (*nee shir laow shir mah;* Are you a teacher?)

The following are some occupations you or the person you're talking with may hold:

- ✔ **biānjí** (*byan jee;* editor)
- ✔ **cáifeng** (*tsye fung;* tailor)
- ✔ **chéngwùyuán** (*chuhng woo ywan;* flight attendant)
- ✔ **chūnàyuán** (*choo nah ywan;* bank teller)
- ✔ **diàngōng** (*dyan goong;* electrician)
- ✔ **fēixíngyuán** (*fay sheeng ywan;* pilot)
- ✔ **hǎiguān guānyuán** (*hi gwan gwan ywan;* Customs agent)
- ✔ **hùshì** (*hoo shir;* nurse)
- ✔ **jiàoshòu** (*jyaow show;* professor)
- ✔ **jiēxiànyuán** (*jyeh shyan ywan;* telephone operator)

- **kèfáng fúwùyuán** (*kuh fahng foo woo ywan;* housekeeper)
- **kuàijì** (*kwye jee;* accountant)
- **lăoshī** (*laow shir;* teacher)
- **lièchēyuán** (*lyeh chuh ywan;* train conductor)
- **lǜshī** (*lyew shir;* lawyer)
- **qiántái fúwùyuán** (*chyan tye foo woo ywan;* receptionist)
- **shuǐnuǎngōng** (*shway nwan goong;* plumber)
- **yǎnyuán** (*yan ywan;* actor)
- **yīshēng** (*ee shung;* doctor)
- **yóudìyuán** (*yo dee ywan;* mail carrier)
- **zhǔguǎn** (*joo gwan;* CEO)

The following are some useful job terms and job-related expressions:

- **bàn rì gōngzuò** (*bahn ir goong dzwaw;* part-time work)
- **gùyuán** (*goo ywan;* employee)
- **gùzhǔ** (*goo joo;* employer)
- **jīnglǐ** (*jeeng lee;* manager)
- **miànshì** (*myan shir;* interview)
- **quán rì gōngzuò** (*chwan ir goong dzwaw;* full-time work)
- **shīyè** (*shir yeh;* unemployed)

In China, your **dānwèi** (*dahn way;* work unit) is an important part of your life. (This term refers to your place of work, which can be anywhere in the country. Your **dānwèi** is the group that's responsible for both taking care of you and being responsible for any missteps you happen to make.) In fact, when people ask you to identify yourself over the phone, they often say **"Nǐ nǎr?"** (*nee nar; literally:* Where are you from?) to find out what **dānwèi** you belong to.

The following dialog uses these occupational phrases:

Xiǎo Liú: **Yáng, nǐ zuò shénme gōngzuò?** (*Yahng, nee dzwaw shummuh goong dzwaw;* Yang, what kind of work do you do?)

Yáng: **Wǒ shì lánqiú duìyuán.** (*waw shir lahn chyo dway ywan;* I'm a basketball player.)

Xiǎo Liú: **Nà hěn yǒuyìsi.** (*nah hun yo ee suh;* That's very interesting.)

Yáng: **Nǐ ne?** (*nee nuh;* How about you?)

Xiǎo Liú: **Wǒ shì hùshì. Wǒ zài Kāifēng dìyī yīyuàn gōngzuò.** (*waw shir hoo shir. waw dzye kye fung dee ee ee ywan goong dzwaw;* I'm a nurse. I work at Kaifeng's No. 1 Hospital.)

Yáng: **Nán bùnán?** (*nahn boo nahn;* Is it difficult?)

Xiǎo Liú: **Bùnán. Wǒ hěn xǐhuān wǒde zhíyè.** (*noo nahn. waw hun she hwahn waw duh jir yeh;* It's not difficult. I really like my profession.)

Words to Know

gōngzuò	goong dzwaw	to work
hùshì	hoo shir	nurse
nán	nahn	difficult
xǐhuān	she hwahn	to like; to enjoy
yīyuàn	ee ywan	hospital
zhíyè	jir yeh	profession

Talking about where you live

After folks get to know each other through small talk, they may exchange addresses and phone numbers to keep in touch. That introductory question covered earlier in this chapter, **"Nǐ zhù zài nǎr?"** (*nee joo dzye nar;* Where do you live?), may pop up. You may also want to ask a few of these questions:

- ✔ **Nǐde dìzhǐ shì shénme?** (*nee duh dee jir shir shummuh;* What's your address?)
- ✔ **Nǐde diànhuà hàomǎ duōshǎo?** (*nee duh dyan hwah how mah dwaw shaow;* What's your phone number?)
- ✔ **Nǐ shénme shíhòu zài jiā?** (*nee shummuh shir ho dzye jyah;* When will you be at home?/When are you home?)

You may also talk about your home from time to time. These words and phrases can come in handy:

- ✔ **Wǒmen zhù de shì fángzi.** (*waw mun joo duh shir fahng dzuh;* We live in a house.)
- ✔ **Tā zhù de shì gōngyù.** (*tah joo duh shir guh goong yew;* She lives in an apartment.)
- ✔ **Tāmen yǒu yíge yuànzi.** (*tah mun yo ee guh ywan dzuh;* They have a yard.)
- ✔ **Nǐ yǒu yíge huāyuán.** (*nee yo ee guh hwah ywan;* You have a garden.)
- ✔ **Wǒ zhù zài chénglǐ.** (*waw joo dzye chuhng lee;* I live in the city.)
- ✔ **Wǒ zhù zài jiāowài.** (*waw joo dzye jyaow why;* I live in the suburbs.)
- ✔ **Wǒ zhù zài nóngcūn.** (*waw joo dzye noong tswun;* I live in the country.)

In addition to your **diànhuà hàomǎ** (*dyan hwah how mah;* phone number) and your **dìzhǐ** (*dee jir;* address), most people also want to know your **diànzǐ yóuxiāng dìzhǐ** (*dyan dzuh yo shyahng dee jir;* e-mail address). And if you find yourself in a more formal situation, it may be appropriate to give someone your **míngpiàn** (*meeng pyan;* business card).

Chapter 5

Enjoying a Drink and a Snack (or Meal!)

• •

In This Chapter

▶ Eating, Chinese style

▶ Ordering and conversing in restaurants

▶ Paying for your meal

• •

*E*xploring Chinese food and Chinese eating etiquette is a great way to discover Chinese culture. You can also use what you discover in this chapter to impress your date by ordering in Chinese the next time you eat out.

All about Meals

If you feel hungry when beginning this section, then stop and **chī** (*chir;* eat) some **fàn** (*fahn;* food). Different meals throughout the day, for example, are called

▶ **zǎofàn** (*dzaow fahn;* breakfast)

▶ **wǔfàn** (*woo fahn;* lunch)

▶ **wǎnfàn** (*wahn fahn;* dinner)

For centuries, Chinese people greeted each other not by saying **"Nǐ hǎo ma?"** (*nee how ma;* How are you?), but by saying **"Nǐ chīfàn le méiyǒu?"** (*nee chir fahn luh mayo; literally:* "Have you eaten?")

If you're hungry, you can say **wǒ hěn è** (*waw hun uh;* I'm very hungry) and wait for a friend to invite you for a bite to eat. If you're thirsty, just say **wǒde kǒu hěn kě** (*waw duh ko hun kuh; literally:* my mouth is very dry) to hear offers for all sorts of drinks.

Or you can be subtler with one of these phrases:

- **Nǐ è ma?** (*nee uh mah;* Are you hungry?)
- **Nǐ è bú è?** (*nee uh boo uh;* Are you hungry?)
- **Nǐ hái méi chī wǎnfàn ba.** (*nee hi may chir wahn fahn bah;* I bet you haven't had dinner yet.)

When having dinner at someone's home, don't be hesitant to use some of these phrases at the table:

- **Màn chī** or **màn màn chī!** (*mahn chir or mahn mahn chir;* Bon appetite!) This phrase literally means "Eat slowly," but it's loosely translated as "Take your time and enjoy your food."
- **Zìjǐ lái.** (*dzuh jee lye;* I'll help myself.)
- **Gānbēi!** (*gahn bay;* Bottoms up!)
- **Duō chī yìdiǎr ba!** (*dwaw chir ee dyar bah;* Have some more!)
- **Wǒ chībǎo le.** (*waw chir baow luh;* I'm full.)

Whenever a dining partner begins to serve you food, as is the custom, you must always feign protest with a few mentions of **zìjǐ lái** (*dzuh jee lye;* I'll help myself) so you don't appear to assume that someone *should* be serving you. In the end, permit the person to follow proper etiquette by serving you portions from each dish if you're the guest.

Dining Out

Whether you eat in a friend's home or in a fancy Chinese restaurant, you need to know how to ask for some basic utensils and how to refer to items already on the table.

You ask for something politely by saying **Qǐng nǐ gěi wǒ . . .** (*cheeng nee gay waw;* Would you mind please getting me a . . .)

You can also say **Máfan nǐ gěi wǒ . . .** (*mah fahn nee gay waw;* May I trouble you to please get me a . . .)

Here are some items you commonly encounter or need to ask for when dining out:

- **yíge wǎn** (*ee guh wahn;* a bowl)
- **yíge pánzi** (*ee guh pahn dzuh;* a plate)
- **yíge bēizi** (*ee guh bay dzuh;* a glass)
- **yíge tiáogēng** (*ee guh tyaow guhng;* a spoon)
- **yíge dāozi** (*ee guh daow dzuh;* a knife)
- **yíge chāzi** (*ee guh chah dzuh;* a fork)
- **yì zhāng cānjīn** (*ee jahng tsahn jeen;* a napkin)
- **yì gēn yáqiān** (*ee gun yah chyan;* a toothpick)
- **yíge shī máojīn** (*ee guh shir maow jeen;* a wet towel)
- **yíge rè máojīn** (*ee guh ruh maow jeen;* a hot towel)
- **yì shuāng kuàizi** (*ee shwahng kwye dzuh;* a pair of chopsticks)

When in doubt, use the measure word **ge** (*guh*) in front of the noun you want to modify by a numeral or a specifier, such as "this" (**zhè;** *jay*) or "that" (**nà;** *nah*). As you can see from the previous list, the word for "a" always begins with **yī** (*ee*), meaning the number 1 in Chinese. In between **yī** and the noun is the measure word. For chopsticks, it's **shuāng** (*shwahng*), meaning pair; for napkin, it's **zhāng** (*jahng*), used for anything with a flat surface (such as paper, a map, or even a bed); and a toothpick's measuring word is **gēn** (*gun*), referring to anything resembling a stick, such as rope, a thread, or a blade of grass. Chinese has many different measure words, but **ge** (*guh*) is by far the most common.

When you're thinking about dining out, here's a conversation you may have:

Livia: **Charlotte, nǐ hǎo!** (*Charlotte, nee how;* Charlotte, hi!*)

Charlotte: **Nǐ hǎo. Hǎo jiǔ méi jiàn.** (*nee how. how jyoe may jyan;* Hi there. Long time no see.)

Livia: **Nǐ è bú è?** (*nee uh boo uh;* Are you hungry?)

Charlotte: **Wǒ hěn è. Nǐ ne?** (*waw hun uh. nee nuh;* Yes, very hungry. How about you?)

Livia: **Wǒ yě hěn è.** (*waw yeah hun uh;* I'm also pretty hungry.)

Charlotte: **Wǒmen qù Zhōngguóchéng chī Zhōngguó cài, hǎo bù hǎo?** (*waw men chyew joong gwaw chuhng chir joong gwaw tsye, how boo how;* Let's go to Chinatown and have Chinese food, okay?)

Livia: **Hǎo. Nǐ zhīdào Zhōngguóchéng nǎ jiā cānguǎn hǎo ma?** (*how. nee jir daow joong gwaw chuhng nah jya tsahn gwahn how ma;* Okay. Do you know which restaurant in Chinatown is good?)

Charlotte: **Běijīng kǎo yā diàn hǎoxiàng bú cuò.** (*bay jeeng cow ya dyan how shyang boo tswaw;* The Peking Duck place seems very good.)

Understanding What's on the Menu

Familiarize yourself with the basic types of food on the **càidān** (*tsye dahn;* menu) in case you have only Chinese characters and pinyin romanization to go on. Having the knowledge allows you to immediately know which section to focus on (or, likewise, to avoid).

Table 5-1 shows the typical elements of a **càidān**:

Table 5-1	Typical Sections of a Chinese Menu	
Chinese Word(s)	**Pronunciation**	**English Word(s)**
kāiwèipǐn	kye way peen	appetizers
ròu lèi	row lay	meat dishes
jī lèi	jee lay	poultry dishes
hǎixiān	hi shyan	seafood dishes
sùcài	soo tsye	vegetarian dishes
tāng	tahng	soup
diǎnxīn	dyan sheen	desserts
yǐnliào	een lyaow	drinks

The following is a conversation you may have when arriving at a restaurant:

Host: **Jǐ wèi?** (*jee way;* How many are in your party?)

Leslie: **Sān wèi.** (*sahn way;* There are three of us.)

Host: **Qǐng zuò zhèr. Zhè shì càidān.** (*cheeng dzwaw jar. jay shir tsye dahn;* Please sit here. Here's the menu.)

Leslie: **Nǐ yào chī fàn háishì yào chī miàn?** (*nee yaow chir fahn hi shir yaow chir myan;* Do you want to eat rice or noodles?)

Gerry: **Liǎngge dōu kéyǐ.** (*lyahng guh doe kuh yee;* Either one is fine.)

Jean: **Wǒ hěn xǐhuān yāoguǒ jīdīng. Nǐmen ne?** (*waw hun she hwan yaow gwaw jee deeng. nee men nuh;* I love diced chicken with cashew nuts. How about you guys?)

Gerry: **Duìbùqǐ, wǒ chī sù. Wǒmen néng bù néng diǎn yìdiǎr dòufù?** (*dway boo chee, waw chir soo. waw mun nung boo nung dyan ee dyar doe foo;* Sorry, I'm a vegetarian. Can we order some tofu?)

Jean: **Dāngrán kěyǐ.** (*dahng rahn kuh yee;* Of course we can.)

Leslie: **Bù guǎn zěnme yàng, wǒmen lái sān píng jiǔ, hǎo bù hǎo?** (*boo gwahn dzummuh yahng, waw mun lye san peeng jyoe, how boo how;* No matter what, let's get three bottles of beer, okay?)

Gerry: **Hěn hǎo!** (*hun how;* Very good!)

Words to Know

bù guǎn zěnme yàng	boo gwahn dzummuh yahng	no matter what
fànguǎn	fahn gwahn	restaurant
gāojí jiǔlóu	gaow jee jyoe low	fancy restaurant
kāfēitīng	kah fay teeng	cafe
kuàicān	kwye tsahn	fast food
píjiǔ	pee jyoe	beer
xiǎochīdiàn	shyaow chir dyan	snack shop
Xīcān	she tsahn	Western food
Zhōngcān	joong tsahn	Chinese food

Vegetarian's delight

If you're a vegetarian, you may feel lost when looking at a menu filled with mostly pork (the staple meat of China), beef, and fish dishes. Not to worry. Table 5-2 shows some vegetarian dishes. (And take a look at the list of vegetables in Chapter 6 for some added help.)

Table 5-2	Vegetarian Dishes	
Chinese Words	*Pronunciation*	*English Words*
dànhuā tāng	dahn hwah tahng	egg drop soup
gānbiān sìjìdòu	gahn byan suh jee doe	sautéed string beans
hóngshāo dòufu	hoong shaow doe foo	braised bean curd in soy sauce
suān là tāng	swan lah tahng	hot-and-sour soup
yúxiāng qiézi	yew shyang chyeh dzuh	spicy eggplant with garlic

Some favorite Chinese dishes

You may be familiar with many of the following dishes if you've ever been in a Chinese restaurant:

- ✔ **Běijīng kǎo yā** (*bay jeeng cow yah;* Peking roast duck)
- ✔ **chūnjuǎn** (*chwun jwan;* spring roll)
- ✔ **dànhuā tāng** (*dahn hwah tahng;* egg drop soup)
- ✔ **dòufu gān** (*doe foo gahn;* dried beancurd)
- ✔ **gàilán niúròu** (*guy lahn nyoe row;* beef with broccoli)
- ✔ **gōngbǎo jīdīng** (*goong baow jee deeng;* diced chicken with hot peppers)
- ✔ **háoyóu niúròu** (*how yo nyoe row;* beef with oyster sauce)
- ✔ **hóngshāo dòufu** (*hoong shaow doe foo;* braised beancurd in soy sauce)
- ✔ **húndùn tāng** (*hwun dwun tahng;* wonton soup)
- ✔ **shuàn yángròu** (*shwahn yahng row;* Mongolian lamb hot pot)

✔ **suān là tāng** (*swan lah tahng;* hot-and-sour soup)

✔ **tángcù yú** (*tahng tsoo yew;* sweet and sour fish)

✔ **yān huánggguā** (*yan hwahng gwah;* pickled cucumber)

Sauces and seasonings

The Chinese use all kinds of seasonings and sauces to make their dishes so tasty. Check out *Chinese Cooking For Dummies* by Martin Yan (Wiley) for much more info. Here are just a few of the basics:

✔ **cù** (*tsoo;* vinegar)

✔ **jiāng** (*jyahng;* ginger)

✔ **jiàngyóu** (*jyahng yo;* soy sauce)

✔ **làyóu** (*lah yo;* hot sauce)

✔ **máyóu** (*mah yo;* sesame oil)

✔ **yán** (*yan;* salt)

Dipping into some dim sum

Dim sum takes the shape of mini portions, and it's often served with tea to help cut through the oil and grease afterwards. Part of the allure of dim sum is that you get to sample a whole range of different tastes while you catch up with old friends. Dim sum meals can last for hours, which is why most Chinese people choose the weekends to have dim sum. No problem lingering on a Saturday or Sunday.

You can tell the waiter you want a specific kind of dim sum by saying:

Qǐng lái yì dié _____. (*cheeng lye ee dyeh _____;* please give me a plate of _____). Fill in the blank with one of the tasty choices I list in Table 5-3.

Table 5-3	Common Dim Sum Dishes	
Chinese Word(s)	**Pronunciation**	**English Word(s)**
chūnjuǎn	chwun jwan	spring rolls
dàntǎ	dahn tah	egg tarts
dòushā bāo	doe shah baow	sweet bean buns
guō tiē	gwaw tyeh	fried pork dumplings
luóbo gāo	law baw gaow	turnip cake
niàng qīngjiāo	nyahng cheeng jyaow	stuffed peppers
niúròu wán	nyoe row wahn	beef balls
yùjiǎo	yew jyaow	deep fried taro root
xiā jiǎo	shyah jyaow	shrimp dumplings
xiā wán	shyah wahn	shrimp balls
xiǎolóng bāo	shyaow lonog baow	steamed pork buns

The following conversation uses these dim sum phrases:

George: **Nǐ chī guò dim sum ma?** (*nee chir gwaw deem sum mah;* Have you ever had dim sum before?)

Rhoda: **Méiyǒu. Zhè shì dì yī cì.** (*mayo. jay shir dee yee tsuh;* No. This is the first time.)

Susan: **Wèidào zěnme yàng?** (*way daow dzum-muh yahng;* How does it taste?)

Rhoda: **Hǎo jíle.** (*how jee luh;* It's great.)

George: **Nǐ xǐ bùxǐhuān chī dim sum?** (*nee she boo she hwahn chir deem sum;* Do you like dim sum?)

Susan: **Dāngrán. Hěn xǐhuān.** (*dahng rahn. hun she hwahn;* Absolutely. I like it very much.)

Rhoda: **Nǐ zuì xǐhuān chī de dim sum shì shénme?** (*nee dzway she hwahn chir duh deem sum shir shummuh;* What's your favorite dim sum dish?)

Susan: **Nà hěn nán shuō. Bú shì guō tiē jiù shì xiā jiǎo ba. Dim sum wǒ dōu xǐhuān chī.** (*nah hun nahn shwaw. boo shir gwaw tyeh jyoe shir shyah jyaow bah. deem sum waw doe she hwahn chir;* It's difficult to say. If not pork dumplings, then definitely shrimp dumplings. I love all dim sum dishes.)

Ordering Western food

Even though Chinese food is so varied and great, once in a while you may really find yourself hankering for a good old American hamburger or a stack of French fries. Table 5-4 lists some items you may want to order when you're in need of some old-fashioned comfort food, and Table 5-5 lists common beverages.

Table 5-4	Western Food	
Chinese Word(s)	*Pronunciation*	*English Word(s)*
bǐsā bǐng	bee sah beeng	pizza
hànbǎobāo	hahn baow baow	hamburger
kǎo tǔdòu	cow too doe	baked potato
règǒu	ruh go	hot dog
sānmíngzhì	sahn meeng jir	sandwich
shālā jiàng	shah lah jyahng	salad dressing

Chinese Word(s)	Pronunciation	English Word(s)
shālā zìzhùguì	shah lah dzuh joo gway	salad bar
tǔdòuní	too doe nee	mashed potatoes
yáng pái	yahng pye	lamb chops
yìdàlì shì miàntiáo	ee dah lee shir myan tyaow	spaghetti
zhá jǐ	jah jee	fried chicken
zhá shǔtiáo	jah shoo tyaow	French fries
zhá yángcōng quān	jah yahng tsoong chwan	onion rings
zhū pái	joo pye	pork chops

Table 5-5	Beverages	
Chinese Word(s)	Pronunciation	English Word(s)
chá	chah	tea
guǒzhǐ	gwaw jir	fruit juice
jiǔdān	jyoe dahn	wine list
kāfēi	kah fay	coffee
kělè	kuh luh	soda
kuàngquánshuǐ	kwahng chwan shway	mineral water
níngmén qìshuǐ	neeng muhng chee shway	lemonade
niúnǎi	nyoe nye	milk
píjiǔ	pee jyoe	beer

Placing an Order and Chatting with the Wait Staff

Chinese table etiquette dictates that everyone decides together what to order. The two main categories you must decide upon are the **cài** (*tsye;* food dishes) and the **tāng** (*tahng;* soup). Feel free to be the first one to ask **wǒmen yīnggāi jiāo jǐge cài jǐge tāng?** (*waw men eeng gye jyaow jee guh tsye jee guh tahng;* How many dishes and how many soups should we order?). Ideally, one of each of the five major tastes should appear in the dishes you choose for your meal to be a "true" Chinese meal: **suān** (*swan;* sour), **tián** (*tyan;* sweet), **kǔ** (*koo;* bitter), **là** (*lah;* spicy), or **xián** (*shyan;* salty).

Here are some questions your server is likely to ask you:

- ✔ **Nǐmen yào shénme cài?** (*nee men yaow shummuh tsye;* What would you like to order? *Literally:* What kind of food would you like?)

- ✔ **Nǐmen yào hē diǎr shénme?** (*nee mun yaow huh dyar shummuh;* What would you like to drink?)

- ✔ **Yào jǐ píng píjiǔ?** (*yaow jee peeng pee jyoe;* How many bottles of beer do you want?)

And here are some phrases that come in handy when you need to give an answer:

- ✔ **Wǒmen yào yíge suān là tāng.** (*waw mun yaow ee guh swan lah tahng;* We'd like a hot-and-sour soup.)

- ✔ **Wǒ bù chī là de.** (*waw boo chir lah duh;* I don't eat spicy food.)

- ✔ **Qǐng bié fàng wèijīng, wǒ guòmǐn.** (*cheeng byeh fahng way jeeng, waw gwaw meen;* Please don't use any MSG, I'm allergic.)

When addressing a food server, you can call him or her by the same name: **fúwùyuán** (*foo woo ywan;* service personnel). In fact, "he," "she," and "it" all share the same Chinese word, too: **tā** (*tah*). Isn't that easy to remember?

- ✔ **Qǐng gěi wǒ càidān.** (*cheeng gay waw tsye dahn;* Please give me the menu.)

- ✔ **Nǐ gěi wǒmen jièshào jǐge cài, hǎo ma?** (*nee gay waw men jyeh shaow gee guh tsye, how ma;* Can you recommend some dishes?)

- ✔ **Dà shīfu náshǒu cài shì shénme?** (*dah shir foo nah show tsye shir shummuh;* What's the chef's specialty?)

- ✔ **Yú xīnxiān ma?** (*yew shin shyan mah;* Is the fish fresh?)

- ✔ **Wǒ bú yuànyì chī hǎishēn.** (*waw boo ywan yee chir hi shun;* I don't want to try sea slugs.)

- ✔ **Nǐmen yǒu kuàngquán shuǐ ma?** (*nee mun yo kwahng chwan shway mah;* Do you have any mineral water?)

- ✔ **Wǒ bú yào là de cài.** (*waw boo yaow lah duh tsye;* I don't want anything spicy.)

- ✔ **Wǒ bù néng chī yǒu táng de cài.** (*waw boo nuhng chir yo tahng duh tsye;* I can't eat anything made with sugar.)

- ✔ **Wǒ bù chī zhūròu.** (*waw boo chir joo row;* I don't eat pork.)

- ✔ **Qǐng cā zhuōzi.** (*cheeng tsah jwaw dzuh;* Please wipe off the table.)

- ✔ **Qǐng bǎ yǐnliào sòng lái.** (*cheeng bah yin lyaow soong lye;* Please bring our drinks.)

- ✔ **Wǒ méi jiào zhèige.** (*waw may jyaow jay guh;* I didn't order this.)

Here's how a conversation may go when ordering:

Tom: **Wǒmen néng bùnéng kànkàn càidān?**
(*waw mun nung boo nung kahn kahn tsye dahn;* May we see the menu?)

Waiter: **Dāngrán kéyǐ.** (*dahng rahn kuh yee;* Of course you may.)

Waiter: **Nǐmen xiǎng diǎn shénme cài?** (*nee mun shyang dyan shummuh tsye;* What dishes would you like to order?)

Tom: **Qǐng wèn, nǐmen de náshǒu cài shì shénme?** (*cheeng one, nee mun duh nah show tsye shir shummuh;* Excuse me, may I ask what your house specialty is?)

Waiter: **Mápó dòufu hé Chángshā jī dōu yǒumíng.** (*mah paw doe foo huh chahng shah jee doe yo meeng;* Sichuan beancurd and Changsha chicken are both very famous.)

Wendy: **Tīngshuō mápó dòufu hěn là. Duìbùqǐ, kěshì wǒ bùchī là de. Yǒu méiyǒu biéde cài?** (*teeng shwaw mah paw doe foo hun lah. dway boo chee, kuh shir waw boo chir lah duh. yo mayo byeh duh tsye;* I've heard the Sichuan beancurd is very spicy. I'm sorry, but I don't like spicy food. Do you have any other kinds of dishes?)

Waiter: **Dāngrán yǒu. Jièlán jī hé xiā lóng hú dōu bǐjiǎo wēnhé. Hǎo bùhǎo?** (*dahng rahn yo. jyeh lahn jee huh shyah loong hoo doe bee jyaow one huh. how boo how;* Of course we do. Chicken with broccoli and shrimp with lobster sauce are both relatively mild. How about those?)

Wendy: **Hěn hǎo. Xièxiè.** (*hun how. shyeh shyeh;* Very good. Thank you.)

Tom: **Qǐng lìngwài gěi wǒmen làjiāo jiàng. Wǒ hěn xǐhuān chī làde.** (*cheeng leeng wye gay waw mun lah jyaow jyahng. waw hun she hwan chir lah duh;* Please also bring us some hot pepper sauce. I love spicy food.)

Waiter: **Hái yào biéde ma?** (*hi yaow byeh duh ma;* Would you like anything else?)

Tom: **Qǐng lìngwài lái yíge chǎo qīngcài.** (*cheeng leeng wye lye ee guh chaow cheeng tsye;* Please also bring a sautéed green vegetable.)

Words to Know

guòmǐn	gwaw meen	allergic
náshǒu cài	nah show tsye	house specialty
tuījiàn	tway jyan	recommend
wèijīng	way jeeng	MSG
Wǒde kǒu hěn kě.	waw duh ko hun kuh	I'm thirsty.
Wǒ hěn è.	waw hun uh	I'm very hungry.

Finding the Restrooms

After you have a bite to eat, you may be in need of a restroom. The need may be dire if you're smack in the middle of a 12-course banquet in Beijing and already had a couple of glasses of **máotái** (*maow tye*), the stiffest of all Chinese drinks.

Now all you have to do is garner the energy to ask **"Cèsuǒ zài nǎr?"** (*tsuh swaw dzye nar;* Where's the restroom?) if you're in mainland China or **"Cèsuǒ zài nǎlǐ?"** (*tsuh swaw dzye nah lee*) if you're in Taiwan. You can also ask **"Nǎlǐ kéyǐ xǐ shǒu?** (*nah lee kuh yee she show;* Where can I wash my hands?)

In most cases, the pictures on the bathroom doors are self-explanatory, but you may also see the pinyin for male (**nán**; *nahn*) and female (**nǚ**; *nyew*) before the word **cèsuǒ**. Those are the words you want to pay attention to above all else.

Finishing Your Meal and Paying the Bill

After you're through sampling all possible permutations of Chinese cuisine, you need to pay the bill, my friend. I hope the food was worth the expense. Here are some phrases you need to know when the time comes:

- **Bāokuò fúwùfèi.** (*baow kwaw foo woo fay;* The tip is included.)

- **fēnkāi suàn** (*fun kye swahn;* to go Dutch)

- **jiézhàng** (*jyeh jahng;* to pay the bill)

- **Qǐng jiézhàng**. (*cheeng jyeh jahng;* The check, please.)

- **Qǐng kāi shōujù.** (*cheeng kye show jyew;* Please give me the receipt.)

- **Wǒ kéyǐ yòng xìnyòng kǎ ma?** (*waw kuh yee yoong sheen yoong kah mah;* May I use a credit card?)

- **Wǒ qǐng kè.** (*waw cheeng kuh;* It's on me.)

- **Zhàngdān bāokuò fúwùfēi ma?** (*jahng dahn baow kwaw foo woo fay mah;* Does the bill include a service charge/tip?)

- **Zhàngdān yǒu cuò.** (*jahng dahn yo tswaw;* The bill is incorrect.)

The following is a short conversation about paying a tip:

Rebecca: **Wǒmen de zhàngdān yígòng sānshí kuài qián. Xiǎo fèi yǐnggāi duōshǎo?** (*waw mun duh jahng dahn ee goong sahn shir kwye chyan. shyaow fay eeng guy dwaw shaow;* Our bill comes to $30 altogether. How much should the tip be?)

Rachel: **Yīnwèi fúwù hěn hǎo, suǒyǐ xiǎo fèi kéyǐ bǎi fēn zhī èr shí. Nǐ tóngyì ma?** (*een way foo woo hun how, swaw yee shyaow fay kuh yee bai fun jir are shir. nee toong ee mah;* Because the service was really good, I think we can leave a 20 percent tip. Do you agree?)

Rebecca: **Tóngyì.** (*toong ee;* I agree.)

All the Tea in China

You encounter about as many different kinds of tea as you do Chinese dialects. Hundreds, in fact. To make ordering or buying this beverage easier, however, you really only need to know the most common kinds of tea:

- ✔ **Lǜ chá.** (*lyew chah;* Green tea) Green tea is the oldest of all the teas in China, with many unfermented subvarieties. The most famous kind of Green tea is called **lóngjǐng chá** (*loong jeeng chah*), meaning Dragon Well tea. You can find it near the famous West Lake region in Hangzhou, and people in the south generally prefer this kind of tea.

- ✔ **Hóng chá.** (*hoong chah;* Black tea) Even though **hóng** means red in Chinese, you translate this phrase as Black tea. Unlike Green tea, Black teas are fermented and enjoyed primarily by people in Fujian Province.

- ✔ **Wūlóng chá.** (*oo loong chah;* Black dragon tea) This kind of tea is semifermented. It's a favorite in Guangdong and Fujian provinces and in Taiwan.

- ✔ **Mòlì huā chá.** (*maw lee hwah chah;* Jasmine) This kind of tea consists of a combination of Black, Green, and Wūlóng teas, in addition to some fragrant flowers like jasmine or magnolia thrown in for good measure. Most northerners are partial to jasmine tea, probably because the north is cold and this type of tea raises the body's temperature.

Chapter 6

Shop 'til You Drop!

• •

In This Chapter

▶ Checking out the stores

▶ Looking for clothes and other items

▶ Bargaining for a better price

▶ Making comparisons

• •

*T*o **mǎi dōngxi** (*my doong she;* buy things) is one of the most enjoyable pastimes for people the world over. Whether you're just going **guàngshāngdiàn** (*gwahng shahng dyan;* window shopping) or actually about to **mǎi dōngxi** doesn't matter. You can still enjoy looking at all the **shāngpǐn** (*shahng peen;* merchandise), fantasizing about buying that **zuànshí jièzhi** (*dzwan shir jyeh jir;* diamond ring), and haggling over the **jiàgé** (*jyah guh;* price).

Going to Stores

The following list contains some types of stores you may encounter and some items you can find in them:

> ✔ **Zài yíge shūdiàn nǐ kéyǐ mǎi shū, zázhì hé bàozhǐ.** (*dzye ee guh shoo dyan nee kuh yee my shoo, dzah jir huh baow jir;* In a bookstore, you can buy books, magazines, and newspapers.)
>
> ✔ **Zài yíge wǔjīn diàn nǐ kéyǐ mǎi zhuǎnjiē qì, chātóu hé yānwù bàojǐng qì.** (*dzye ee guh woo jeen dyan nee kuh yee my jwan jyeh chee, chah*

toe huh yan woo baow jeeng chee; In a hardware store, you can buy adaptors, plugs, and smoke detectors.)

✔ **Zài yíge yāncǎo diàn nǐ kéyǐ mǎi xuějiāyān, xiāngyān, yāndǒu hé gèzhǒng gèyàng de yāncǎo.** (*dzye ee guh yan tsaow dyan nee kuh yee my shyweh jyah yan, shyahng yan, yan doe huh guh joong guh yahng duh yan tsaow;* In a tobacco shop, you can buy cigars, cigarettes, pipes, and all kinds of tobacco.)

✔ **Zài yíge zhūbǎo diàn nǐ kéyǐ mǎi shǒuzhuó, ěrhuán, xiàngliàn, xiōngzhēn hé jièzhi.** (*dzye ee guh joo baow dyan nee kuh yee my show jwaw, are hwahn, shyahng lyan, shyoong juhn huh jyeh jir;* In a jewelry store, you can buy bracelets, earrings, necklaces, pins, and rings.)

Here are a few other stores you may want to visit:

✔ **bǎihuò shāngdiàn** (*bye hwaw shahng dyan;* department stores)

✔ **chàngpiàn diàn** (*chahng pyan dyan;* record store)

✔ **chāojí shìchǎng** (*chow jee shir chahng;* supermarket)

✔ **fúzhuāng diàn** (*foo jwahng dyan;* clothing store)

✔ **lǐpǐn diàn** (*lee peen dyan;* gift shop)

✔ **shūdiàn** (*shoo dyan;* bookstore)

✔ **wánjù diàn** (*wahn jyew dyan;* toy store)

✔ **wǔjīn diàn** (*woo jeen dyan;* hardware store)

✔ **xiédiàn** (*shyeh dyan;* shoe store)

✔ **yàofáng** (*yaow fahng;* drugstore)

When you finally make up your mind about what to shop for, you may want to call ahead to check out the store's hours. The following questions can be helpful:

✔ **Nín jǐ diǎn zhōng kāi/guān mén?** (*neen jee dyan joong kye/gwahn mun;* What time do you open/close?)

✔ **Nǐmen wǔdiǎn zhōng yǐhòu hái kāi ma?** (*nee mun woo dyan joong ee hoe hi kye mah;* Are you open after 5 p.m.?)

✔ **Nǐmen xīngqītiān kāi bùkāi?** (*nee mun sheeng chee tyan kye boo kye;* Are you open on Sundays?)

If all you want to do is browse, you don't want a **shòuhuòyuán** (*show hwaw ywan;* salesperson) sneaking up behind you and asking **Nǐ xiǎng mǎi shénme?** (*nee shyahng my shummuh;* What would you like to buy?). At this point, just say **Wǒ zhǐ shì kànkàn. Xièxiè.** (*waw jir shir kahn kahn. shyeh shyeh;* I'm just looking. Thanks.)

But if you really do want help, here are some phrases that can help:

✔ **Néng bùnéng bāngmáng?** (*nung boo nung bahng mahng;* Can you help me?)

✔ **Nǐ yǒu méiyǒu Yīngwén de shū?** (*nee yo mayo eeng one duh shoo;* Do you have any books in English?)

✔ **Nǎr yǒu wàitào?** (*Nar yo why taow;* Where are the jackets?)

✔ **Qǐng nǐ gěi wǒ kànkàn nǐde xīzhuāng.** (*cheeng nee gay waw kahn kahn nee duh she jwahng;* Please show me your [Western] suits.)

✔ **Nǐmen mài búmài guāngpán?** (*nee mun my boo my gwahng pahn;* Do you sell CDs?)

Shopping for Clothes

Going shopping for clothes is an art — one requiring plenty of patience and fortitude, not to mention new vocabulary if you're going to do it in Chinese.

What's your size?

To find the right **dàxiǎo** (*dah shyaow;* size) in Chinese, here are some useful phrases you may want to know:

> ✔ **Nín chuān duō dà hào?** (*neen chwan dwaw dah how;* What size are you?*)
>
> ✔ **Dàxiǎo búduì.** (*dah shyaow boo dway;* It's the wrong size.*)
>
> ✔ **Hěn héshēn.** (*hun huh shun;* It fits really well.*)
>
> ✔ **Zài Měiguó wǒde chǐcùn shì wǔ hào.** (*dzye may gwaw waw duh chir tswun shir woo how;* In America I wear a size 5.*)

Instead of using the word **dàxiǎo**, you can say

> ✔ **Wǒ chuān sānshíqī hào.** (*waw chwahn sahn shir chee how;* I wear a size 37.*)
>
> ✔ **Nín chuān jǐ hào de chènshān?** (*neen chwahn jee how duh chun shahn;* What size shirt do you wear?*)
>
> ✔ **Wǒ chuān xiǎohào.** (*waw chwahn shyaow how;* I wear a size small.*)

Of course, you can always guess your approximate size just by indicating you want to see something in one of the following categories:

> ✔ **xiǎo** (*shyaow;* small)
>
> ✔ **zhōng** (*joong;* medium)
>
> ✔ **dà** (*dah;* large)

Here's a sample conversation using some of these phrases:

Julia: **Wǒ xiǎng mǎi yíjiàn jiákè.** (*waw shyahng my ee jyan jyah kuh;* I'm looking for a jacket.*)

Clerk: **Hǎo ba. Nǐ chuān jǐ hào?** (*how bah. nee chwahn jee how;* Very well. What size are you?*)

Julia: **Wǒ bùzhīdào. Měiguó de hàomǎ hé Zhōngguó de hàomǎ hěn bùyíyàng.** (*waw boo jir daow. may gwaw duh how ma huh joong gwaw duh how ma hun boo ee yahng;* I don't know. American sizes are quite different from Chinese sizes.*)

Clerk: **Wǒ gūjì nǐ chuān xiǎohào.** (*waw goo jee nee chwahn shyaow how;* I would estimate you wear a size small.)

Julia: **Hǎo ba. Nà, máfán nǐ gěi wǒ kànkàn xiǎohào de jiákè. Xièxiè.** (*how bah. nah, mah fahn nee gay waw kahn kahn shyaow how duh jyah kuh. shyeh shyeh;* That sounds about right. Would you mind showing me the small size jackets, then? Thank you.)

Words to Know

chǐcùn	chir tswun	measurement
dàhào	dah how	large
jiādàhào	jyah dah how	extra-large
kuān	kwan	wide
sōng	soong	loose
xiǎohào	shyaow how	small
zhǎi	jye	narrow
zhōnghào	joong how	medium

What are you wearing?
Chuān versus dài

Dài (*dye*) and **chuān** (*chwan*) both mean *to wear*, but Chinese uses them differently depending on what you're putting on your body. You **dài** things like **màozi** (*maow dzuh;* hats) and **yǎnjìng** (*yan jeeng;* glasses) — in other words accessories, but you **chuān** things like **qúnzi** (*chewn dzuh;* skirts) and **dàyī** (*dah ee;* coats).

Here are some things you can **chuān:**

- **bèixīn** (*bay sheen;* vest)
- **chángkù** (*chahng koo;* pants; also referred to simply as kùzi)
- **chángxiù** (*chahng shyoe;* long sleeve)
- **chènshān** (*chun shahn;* blouse)
- **dàyī** (*dah ee;* coat)
- **duǎnkù** (*dwan koo;* shorts)
- **duǎnxiù** (*dwahn shyoe;* short sleeve)
- **jiákè** (*jyah kuh;* jacket)
- **kùzi** (*koo dzuh;* pants)
- **nèiyī** (*nay ee;* underwear)
- **niúzǎikù** (*nyo dzye koo;* blue jeans)
- **qúnzi** (*chewn dzuh;* skirt)
- **tuōxié** (*twaw shyeh;* slippers)
- **wàzi** (*wah dzuh;* socks)
- **yǔyī** (*yew ee;* raincoat)
- **gāogēnxié** (*gaow gun shyeh;* high heels)

Here are some things you **dài:**

- **lǐngdài** (*leeng dye;* necktie)
- **shǒubiǎo** (*show byow;* wristwatch)
- **shǒutào** (*show taow;* gloves)
- **zhūbǎo** (*joo byaow;* jewelry)

Asking about the color

Yánsè (*yan suh;* colors) are an important consideration when buying clothes. Do you generally prefer **dānsè** (*dahn suh;* solid colors) or **huā** (*hwah;* patterned) shirts? The following is a list of handy words the next time you go shopping either for clothes or for material to create your own.

- ✔ **bái** (*bye;* white)
- ✔ **fěnhóng** (*fun hoong;* pink)
- ✔ **hēi** (*hey;* black)
- ✔ **hóng** (*hoong;* red)
- ✔ **huáng** (*hwahng;* yellow)
- ✔ **júhóng** (*jyew hoong;* orange)
- ✔ **lán** (*lahn;* blue)
- ✔ **zǐ** (*dzuh;* purple)
- ✔ **dānsè** (*dahn suh;* solid color)
- ✔ **dàn yìdiǎn** (*dahn ee dyan;* lighter)
- ✔ **duànzi** (*dwahn dzuh;* satin)
- ✔ **huā** (*hwah;* patterned)
- ✔ **kāishìmǐ** (*kye shir mee;* cashmere)
- ✔ **liàozi** (*lyaow dzuh;* fabric)
- ✔ **shēn yìdiǎn** (*shun ee dyan;* darker)
- ✔ **sīchóu** (*suh cho;* silk)
- ✔ **yángmáo** (*yahng maow;* wool)

Here's a conversation that incorporates colors:

Laurel: **Zhè jiàn máoyī nǐ juéde zěnmeyàng?**
(*jay jyan maow ee nee jweh duh dzummuh yahng;*
What do you think of this sweater?*)

John: **Nà jiàn máoyī tài xiǎo. Yánsè yě
búpiàoliàng.** (*nay jyan mow ee tye shyaow. yan
suh yeah boo pyaow lyahng;* That sweater is too
small. The color doesn't look good either.*)

Laurel: **Nǐ xǐhuān shénme yánsè?** (*nee she hwahn
shummuh yan suh;* What color do you like?*)

John: **Wǒ xǐhuān hóngde. Búyào nèige hēide.**
(*waw she hwahn hoong duh. boo yaow nay guh
hey duh;* I like the red one. You shouldn't get the
black one.*)

Laurel: **Hǎole. Nà, wǒ jiù mǎi hóngde ba.** (*how
luh. nah, waw jyo my hoong duh bah;* Okay. In
that case I'll buy the red one.*)

When the possessive particle **de** is attached to an adjective and no noun follows it, it can be translated as *the one which is (adjective)*, as in **hóngde** (*hoong duh;* the red one), **dà de** (*dah duh;* the big one), **tián de** (*tyan duh;* the sweet one), and so on.

You can use two classifiers when it comes to clothing: **jiàn** and **tiáo.** Classifiers are the words used in between a number or the words *this* or *that* and the clothing you're talking about. **Jiàn** is used when you're talking about clothing worn on the upper part of the body, and **tiáo** is used for clothes worn on the lower part. So you'd say **yíjiàn chènshān** (*ee jyan chun shahn;* one shirt) or **sāntiáo kùzi** (*sahn tyaow koo dzuh;* three pairs of pants).

Shopping for Other Items

Of course clothes aren't the only items in the world to buy. How about some antiques or hi-tech toys? The possibilities are endless in today's consumer-oriented world.

Hunting for antiques

One of the best places in the world to go searching for **gǔdǒng** (*goo doong;* antiques) is — you guessed it — China. The following words and phrases can come in handy when hunting for antiques:

- ✔ **Zhè shì něige cháodài de?** (*jay shir nay guh chaow dye duh;* Which dynasty is this from?)

- ✔ **Néng dài chūguó ma?** (*nung dye choo gwaw mah;* Can it be taken out of China?)

- ✔ **Nǐde gǔdǒng dìtǎn zài nǎr?** (*nee duh goo doong dee tahn dzye nar;* Where are your antique carpets?)

✔ **Kéyǐ bùkéyǐ jiā zhǔnxǔ chūguó de huǒqǐ yìn?** (*kuh yee boo kuh yee jyah jwun shyew choo gwaw duh hwaw chee yeen;* Can you put the export seal on it?)

✔ **Zhèige duōshǎo nián?** (*jay guh dwaw shaow nyan;* How old is this?)

✔ **Něige cháodài de?** (*nay guh chaow dye duh?* Which dynasty is it from?)

✔ **bí yān hú** (*bee yan who;* snuff bottles)

✔ **dēnglóng** (*dung loong;* lantern)

✔ **diāokè pǐn** (*dyaow kuh peen;* carved objects)

✔ **fóxiàng** (*faw shyahng;* Buddhas)

✔ **gǔdǒng diàn** (*goo doong dyan;* antique shop)

✔ **gǔdǒng jiājù** (*goo doong jyah jyew;* antique furniture)

✔ **gùizi** (*gway dzuh;* chest)

✔ **jìbài yòng de zhuōzi** (*jee bye yoong duh jwaw dzuh;* altar table)

✔ **jǐngtàilán** (*jeeng tye lahn;* cloisonné)

✔ **píngfēng** (*peeng fung;* screen)

✔ **shénxiàng** (*shun shyahng;* idol)

✔ **shūfǎ** (*shoo fah;* calligraphy)

✔ **xiōngzhēn** (*shyoong juhn;* brooch)

✔ **xiùhuā zhìpǐn** (*shyow hwah jir peen;* embroidery)

✔ **yù** (*yew;* jade)

Buying hi-tech and electronics

New electronic gadgets appear on the market every two minutes these days, or so it seems. The following list includes some of the most commonly used (and most commonly bought) items you may need:

✔ **chuánzhēn jǐ** (*chwahn juhn jee;* fax machine)

✔ **dǎyìnjǐ** (*dah yeen jee;* printer)

✔ **diànnǎo shèbèi** (*dyan now shuh bay;* computer equipment)

✔ **diànshì jī** (*dyan shir jee;* TV)

✔ **gèrén diànnǎo** (*guh run dyan now;* PC)

✔ **guāngpán** (*gwahng pahn;* CD)

✔ **jiànpán** (*jyan pahn;* keyboard)

✔ **jìsuàn jī** (*jee swaan jee;* computer)

✔ **kǎlāōukèi jī** (*kah lah okay jee;* karaoke machine)

✔ **ruǎnjiàn** (*rwahn jyan;* software)

✔ **sǎomiáoyí** (*saow myaow ee;* scanner)

✔ **shèxiàng jī** (*shuh shyahng jee;* camcorder)

✔ **shǒutíshì** (*show tee shir;* laptop)

✔ **shǔbiāo** (*shoe byaow;* mouse)

✔ **xiǎnshìqì** (*shyan shir chee;* monitor)

✔ **yìngjiàn** (*eeng jyan;* computer hardware)

✔ **zǔhé yīnxiǎng** (*dzoo huh yeen shyahng;* stereo system)

Hitting the Markets for Food

Outdoor markets in China usually offer all sorts of food items. Table 6-1 lists them for you:

Table 6-1	Typical Foods	
Chinese Word(s)	**Pronunciation**	**English Word(s)**
ròu	row	meat
niúròu	nyoe row	beef
yángròu	yahng row	lamb
jīròu	jee row	chicken
yú	yew	fish
xiā	shyah	shrimp

Chinese Word(s)	Pronunciation	English Word(s)
pángxiè	pahng shyeh	crab
lóngxiā	loong shyah	lobster
yóuyú	yo yew	squid
shuǐguǒ	shway gwaw	fruit
píngguǒ	peeng gwaw	apples
júzi	jyew dzuh	oranges
biǎndòu	byan doe	string bean
bōcài	baw tsye	spinach
dòufu	doe foo	bean curd
fānqié	fahn chyeh	tomato
gàilán	gye lahn	Chinese broccoli
mógū	maw goo	mushroom
qiézi	chyeh dzuh	eggplant
qīngjiāo	cheeng jyaow	green pepper
tǔdòu	too doe	potato
xīlánhuā	she lahn hwah	broccoli
yáng báicài	yahng bye tsye	cabbage
yùmǐ	yew me	corn
zhúsǔn	joo swoon	bamboo shoot

These following words can be helpful when buying food:

- ✔ **màiròude** (*my row duh;* butcher)
- ✔ **chāojí shìchǎng** (*chow jee shir chahng;* supermarket)
- ✔ **shìchǎng** (*shir chahng;* market)
- ✔ **shípǐn záhuò** (*shir peen dzah hwaw;* groceries)

   ✔ **shòuhuòtān** (_show hwaw tahn;_ stall)

   ✔ **záhuòshāng** (_dzah hwaw shahng;_ grocer)

   ✔ **zhǐ dài** (_jir dye;_ a paper bag)

When buying fruits and vegetables, you buy by the weight, which is the metric system in both mainland China and Taiwan. The basic unit of weight is the **gōngkè** (_goong kuh;_ gram). The standard liquid measurement is the **shēng** (_shung;_ liter). One liter equals about 1.06 quarts. Table 6-2 gives you a list of weights and measures.

Table 6-2	**Weights and Measures**	
Chinese Word	_Pronunciation_	_English Word_
pǐntuō	peen twaw	pint
bàng	bahng	pound
kuātuō	kwah twaw	quart
àngsi	ahng suh	ounce
jiālún	jyah lwun	gallon
gōngkè	goong kuh	gram
gōngjīn	goong jeen	kilogram
háokè	how kuh	milligram
shēng	shung	liter
límǐ	lee mee	centimeter
gōnglǐ	goong lee	kilometer
mǐ	mee	meter
yīnglǐ	eeng lee	mile
mǎ	mah	yard
yīngcùn	eeng tswun	inch
yīngchǐ	eeng chir	foot

Getting a Good Price and Paying

When you're ready to buy some merchandise, here are two simple ways to ask how much the products cost:

✔ **Duōshǎo qián?** (*dwaw shaow chyan;* How much money is it?)

✔ **Jǐkuài qián?** (*jee kwye chyan; literally:* How many dollars does it cost?)

The only difference between the two questions is the implied amount of the cost. If you use the question word "**duōshǎo**" (*dwaw shaow*), you want to inquire about something that's most likely greater than $10. If you use "**jǐ**" in front of **kuài** (*kwye;* the term for dollars), you assume the product costs less than $10. Of course, whether you accept that price depends on where you're shopping.

Negotiating prices at the night market

Among the more fun things to do in Taiwan and mainland China is visit one of the many lively night markets. Because the Chinese love to **mǎi dōngxi** (*my doong she;* shop) and **tǎojià huánjià** (*taow jyah hwahn jyah;* haggle), you'll have plenty of company on your sojourns.

You always need to assume that prices are negotiable in an open-air market. You can always ask one of the following and see what happens:

✔ **Néng bùnéng piányì yìdiǎr?** (*nung boo nung pyan yee ee dyar;* Can you sell it more cheaply?)

✔ **Néng bùnéng shǎo yìdiǎr?** (*nung boo nung shaow ee dyar;* Can you lower the price?)

Or you can always play hardball and say something like **Zěnme zhèmme guì a?** (*dzummah jummah gway ah;* Why is this so expensive?) in an exasperated voice, start walking away and see what happens. These haggling-related phrases are also worth knowing:

✔ **Nǐmen shōu bù shōu Měiyuán?** (*nee mun show boo show may ywan;* Do you accept U.S. dollars?)

✔ **Zhèige duōshǎo qián?** (*jay guh dwaw shaow chyan;* How much is this?)

✔ **Dǎ zhé, hǎo bùhǎo?** (*dah juh, how boo how;* How about giving me a discount?)

✔ **Kéyǐ jiǎng jià ma?** (*kuh yee jyahng jyah mah;* Can we negotiate the price?)

The following conversation uses some of these phrases:

Kate: **Zhè tiáo hóng qúnzi duōshǎo qián?** (*jay tyaow hoong chwun dzuh dwaw shaow chyan;* How much is this red skirt?)

Clerk: **Nà tiáo qúnzi èrshíwǔ kuài qián.** (*nah tyaow chwun dzuh are shir woo kwye chyan;* That skirt is $25.)

Kate: **Nà tài guìle! Nǐ néng bùnéng dǎ zhé?** (*nah tye gway luh. nee nung boo nung dah juh;* That's too expensive! Can you give me a discount?)

Clerk: **Kěnéng.** (*kuh nung.* Perhaps.)

Kate: **Nǐ néng gěi wǒ duōdà de zhékòu?** (*nee nung gay waw dwaw dah duh juh ko;* How much of a discount can you give me?)

Clerk: **Bǎi fēn zhī shí, hǎo bùhǎo?** (*bye fun jir shir, how boo how;* How's 10 percent?)

Kate: **Nà tài hǎo le. Xièxiè.** (*nah tye how luh. shyeh shyeh;* That's great. Thanks.)

Demanding a refund

If you end up being **bùyúkuài** (*boo yew kwye;* unhappy) about your purchase, one of these phrases may come in handy when you try to **tuì** (*tway;* return) your **huò** (*hwaw;* merchandise):

✔ **Wǒ yāoqiú tuìkuǎn.** (*waw yaow chyo tway kwahn;* I want a refund.)

- **Wǒ yào tuì huò.** (*waw yaow tway hwaw;* I would like to return this.)

- **Qǐng nǐ bǎ qián jìrù wǒde xìnyòng kǎ.** (*cheeng nee bah chyan jee roo waw duh sheen yoong kah;* Please refund my credit card.)

- **Wǒ néng bùnéng jiàn zǒngjīnglǐ?** (*waw nung boo nung jyan dzoong jeeng lee;* May I see the manager?)

- **Qǐng nǐ bāo qǐlái.** (*cheeng nee baow chee lye;* Please wrap these/this.)

- **Duì wǒ bù héshēn.** (*dway waw boo huh shun;* It doesn't fit me.)

Comparing Quality: Good, Better, Best

When you want to let loose with a superlative in order to say something is absolutely the best — or, for that matter, the worst — always keep this one little word in mind: **zuì** (*dzway*), which means the most (it's the equivalent of the suffix *-est*).

Zuì is a word just waiting for something to follow it; otherwise it won't have much meaning. Here are some superlatives you may need to use from time to time:

- **zuì lèi** (*dzway lay;* the most tired)

- **zuì màn** (*dzway mahn;* the slowest)

- **zuì máng** (*dzway mahng;* the busiest)

- **zuì qíguài** (*dzway chee gwye;* the strangest)

- **zuì yǒumíng** (*dzway yo meeng;* the most famous)

- **zuì yǒuqián** (*dzway yo chyan;* the richest)

If you just want to say that something is better than something else, or "more" something, rather than the best necessarily, you use the word **gèng** (*guhng*) before an adjective. You can consider these the equivalent of the suffix *-er*. Another word that has the meaning of *more* or *-er* is **yìdiǎn** (*ee dyan*). Although the term **gèng** comes before an adjective, the term **yìdiǎn** must appear after it. Instead of saying **gèng kuài** (*gung kwye;* faster), for example, say **kuài yìdiǎn** (*kwye ee dyan*) to mean *faster.*

Here are some examples:

> ✔ **gèng cōngmíng** (*guhng tsoong meeng;* smarter)
> ✔ **gèng guì** (*guhng gway;* more expensive)
> ✔ **piányi yìdiǎn** (*pyan yee ee dyan;* cheaper)
> ✔ **gèng kuài** (*guhng kwye;* faster)
> ✔ **gèng màn** (*guhng mahn;* slower)
> ✔ **hǎo** (*how;* good)
> ✔ **gèng hǎo** (*guhng how;* better)
> ✔ **zuì hǎo** (*dzway how;* best)
> ✔ **duǎn yìdiǎn** (*dwahn ee dyan;* shorter)
> ✔ **cháng yìdiǎn** (*chahng ee dyan;* longer)
> ✔ **xiǎo yìdiǎn** (*shyaow ee dyan;* smaller)
> ✔ **dà yìdiǎn** (*dah ee dyan;* larger)
> ✔ **gèng piányi** (*gung pyan yee;* cheaper)

When you want to compare people or objects, you generally put the word **bǐ** (*bee;* compared to) between two nouns, followed by an adjective: A **bǐ** B (adjective). This means A is more ____ than B.

Here are a few examples:

> ✔ **Píngguǒ bǐ júzi hǎochī.** (*peeng gwaw bee jyew dzuh how chir;* Apples are tastier than oranges.)
> ✔ **Zhèige fànguǎr bǐ nèige fànguǎr guì.** (*jay guh fahn gwar bee nay guh fahng gwar gway;* This restaurant is more expensive than that one.)
> ✔ **Tā bǐ nǐ niánqīng.** (*tah bee nee nyan cheeng;* She's younger than you.)

If instead you want to convey similarity between two things, use the coverbs **gēn** (*gun*) or **hé** (*huh*) in between the two things being compared, followed by the word **yíyàng** (*ee yahng;* the same) and then the adjective. So if you say A **gēn** B **yíyàng dà** (*A gun B ee yahng dah*), you're saying that A and B are equally large or as big as each other. You can also just say A **gēn** B **yíyàng**, meaning A and B are the same. Here are some other things you can say with this sentence pattern:

> ✔ **Gēge hé dìdi yíyàng gāo.** (*guh guh huh dee dee ee yahng gaow;* My older brother is as tall as my younger brother.

> ✔ **Māo gēn gǒu yíyàng tiáopí.** (*maow gun go ee yahng tyaow pee;* Cats are just as naughty as dogs.)

> ✔ **Wǒ gēn nǐ yíyàng dà.** (*waw gun nee ee yahng dah;* You and I are the same age.)

To make a negative comparison, such as *I'm not as tall as he,* use the following sentence pattern:

> A **méiyǒu** B **nèmme** adjective

The means "A is not as (adjective) as B." You can see this pattern in action in the following sentences:

> ✔ **Shāyú méiyǒu jīnyú nèmme kě'ài.** (*shah yew mayo jeen yew nummah kuh eye;* Sharks are not as cute as goldfish.)

> ✔ **Yīngwén méiyǒu Zhōngwén nèmme nán.** (*eeng one mayo joong one nummah nahn;* English is not as difficult as Chinese.)

> ✔ **Māo de wěiba méiyǒu tùzi de wěiba nèmme cū.** (*maow duh way bah mayo too dzuh duh way bah nummah tsoo;* Cats' tails aren't as thick as the tails of rabbits.)

Here's a dialog using comparisons:

Olivia: **Zhè jiàn qípáo zěnmeyàng?** (*jay jyan chee paow dzummah yahng;* What do you think of this traditional Chinese dress?)

Lěiléi: **Wǒ juéde hěn hǎo.** (*waw jweh duh hun how;* I think it looks great.)

Olivia: **Zhēnde ma?** (*jun duh mah;* Really?)

Lěiléi: **Zhēnde. Kěshì jīnsède méiyǒu hóngde nèmme piàoliàng.** (*jun duh. kuh shir jeen suh duh mayo hoong duh nummah pyaow lyahng;* Really. But the gold one isn't as pretty as the red one.)

Olivia: **Jīnsède hé hóngde yíyàng guì ma?** (*jeen suh duh huh hoong duh ee yahng gway mah;* Are the gold one and the red one the same price?)

Lěiléi: **Méiyǒu. Jīnsède bǐ hóngde piányi.** (*mayo. jeen suh duh bee hoong duh pyan yee;* No. The gold one is less expensive than the red one.)

Olivia: **Nà, wǒ jiù mǎi jīnsède.** (*nah, waw jyoe my jeen suh duh;* In that case I'll buy the gold one.)

Chapter 7

Making Leisure a Top Priority

• •

In This Chapter

▶ Getting into the nightlife

▶ Talking about your hobbies

▶ Appreciating Mother Nature

▶ Exercising as an athlete

• •

L ife requires a little fun, a little going out on the town, a little immersing yourself in a hobby, a little getting outdoors, a little delving into art, and a little playing your favorite sport. This chapter gets you out of the house.

Going Out on the Town

If you have an active nightlife, then you want to review this section thoroughly. It offers you plenty of vocabulary to help you when you're out on the town.

Attending a performance

Are you planning on taking in a few **yǎnchū** (*yan choo; shows*) in the near future? You have so much to choose from nowadays:

✔ **bāléi** (*bah lay; ballet*)

✔ **diànyǐng** (*dyan yeeng; movie*)

✔ **gējù** (*guh jyew;* opera)

✔ **yīnyuèhuì** (*yin yweh hway;* music concert)

The following phrases can help you get what you want, or at least understand what you're being told:

✔ **Zài nǎr kéyǐ mǎidào piào?** (*dzye nar kuh yee my daow pyaow;* Where can I buy tickets?)

✔ **Yǒu méiyǒu jīntiān wǎnshàng yǎnchū de piào?** (*yo mayo jin tyan wahn shahng yan choo duh pyaow;* Are there any tickets to tonight's performance?)

✔ **Duìbùqǐ, jīntiān wǎnshàng de piào dōu màiwán le.** (*dway boo chee, jin tyan wahn shahng duh pyaow doe my wahn luh;* I'm sorry, tickets for tonight are all sold out.)

✔ **Wǒ yào mǎi yì zhāng dàrén piào, liǎng zhāng értóng piào.** (*waw yaow my ee jahng dah run pyaow, lyahng jahng are toong pyaow;* I'd like to buy one adult ticket and two kids' tickets.)

✔ **Shénme shíhòu kāiyǎn?** (*shummuh shir ho kye yan;* What time does the show begin?)

✔ **Shénme shíhòu yǎn wán?** (*shummuh shir ho yan wahn;* What time does the show end?)

You can use these phrases in a conversation like this one:

Maria: **Nǐmen jīntiān wǎnshàng xiǎng kàn shénme? Kàn huàjùma?** (*nee men jin tyan wahn shahng shyahng kahn shummuh? kahn hwah jyew mah;* What do you guys want to see tonight? A play?)

Catherine: **Wǒ hěn xiǎng qù kàn wǔshù biǎoyǎn. Zájì biǎoyǎn yě kéyǐ.** (*waw hun shyahng chyew kahn woo shoo byaow yan. dzah jee byaow yan yeah kuh yee;* I'd really like to see a martial arts performance. Acrobatics would be okay, too.)

Elizabeth: **Wǒ xiǎng kàn huàjù.** (*waw shyahng kahn hwah jyew;* I want to see a play.)

Maria: **Nǐmen kànguò Jīngjù ma?** *nee mun kahn gwaw jeeng jyew mah;* Have you ever seen Peking Opera?)

Catherine: **Méiyǒu.** (*mayo;* No.)

Maria: **Nà, wǒmen qù kàn Jīngjù ba! Jīngjù shénme dōu yǒu. Yǒu huàjù, yǒu wǔshù, lián zájì yě yǒu.** (*nah, waw mun chyew kahn jeeng jyew bah! jeeng jyew shummuh doe yo. hwah jyew yo, woo shoo yo, lyan dzah jee yeah yo;* In that case, let's go to see Peking Opera! It has everything. It has a play, it has martial arts, and it even has acrobatics.)

Maria: **Nǐ hǎo. Wǒ xiǎng mǎi sānzhāng jīntiān wǎnshàng de piào.** (*nee how. waw shyahng my sahn jahng jin tyan wahn shahng duh pyaow;* Hello. I'd like to buy three tickets to tonight's performance.)

Clerk: **Hǎo ba. Jīntiān wǎnshàng de piào chàbùduō dōu màiwán le. Zhǐ yǒu èr lóu de zuòwèi.** (*how bah. jin tyan wahn shahng duh pyaow chah boo dwaw doe my wahn luh. jir yo are low duh dzwaw way;* Sure. Tickets for tonight are almost all sold out. We only have second floor seats left.)

Maria: **èr lóu méiyǒu wèntí. Qián pái zuòwèi de piào yǒu méiyǒu?** (*are low mayo one tee. chyan pye dzwaw way duh pyaow yo mayo;* Second floor is no problem. Do you have any front row seats, though?)

Clerk: **Yǒu. Yígòng sānshí kuài qián.** (*yo. ee goong sahn shir kwye chyan;* Yes. That will be $30 all together.)

Words to Know

bāléi wǔ	bah lay woo	ballet
dìfāng xì	dee fahng she	local folk opera

continued

Words to Know (continued)

gēwǔ	guh woo	song and dance
Jīngjù	jeeng jyew	Peking Opera
jùchǎng	jyew chahng	theater
lǐtáng	lee tahng	auditorium
lóushàng de wèizi	lo shahng duh way dzuh	balcony seats
lóuxià de wèizi	lo shyah duh way dzuh	orchestra seats
mùjiān xiūxi	moo jyan shyo she	intermission
piào	pyaow	tickets
wǔshù biǎoyǎn	woo shoo byaow yan	martial arts performance
yīnyuè tīng	yin yweh teeng	concert hall
Yuèjù	yweh jyew	Cantonese opera
zájì biǎoyǎn	dzah jee byaow yan	acrobatic performance

Exploring museums and galleries

Theater shows and live musical performances aren't the only forms of entertainment you can see to get your fill of **wénhuà** (*one hwah;* culture). One of the nicest, calmest activities to do at your own pace is to visit a **bówùguǎn** (*baw woo gwahn;* museum) or **huàláng** (*hwah lahng;* gallery). Sometimes the best reason to go to a **bówùguǎn** is to buy some **lǐwù** (*lee woo;* gifts) and some cool **zhāotiē** (*jaow tyeh;* posters).

Here are some questions you may want to ask in a museum or gallery:

- ✔ **Bówùguǎn jǐdiǎn zhōng kāimén?** (*baw woo gwahn jee dyan joong kye mun;* What time does the museum open?)

- ✔ **Lǐpǐn shāngdiàn shénme shíhòu guānmén?** (*lee peeng shahng dyan shummuh shir ho gwahn mun;* What time does the gift shop close?)

- ✔ **Nǐmen mài búmài zhāotiē?** (*nee mun my boo my jaow tyeh;* Do you sell posters?)

Words to Know

bówùguǎn	baw woo gwahn	museum
huàláng	hwah lahng	gallery
jiézuò	jyeh dzwaw	masterpiece
shǒuyìrén	show ee run	artisan
yìshù	ee shoo	art
yìshùjiā	ee shoo jyah	artist

Visiting historical sites

By far the easiest way to see the major historical sites in China is to join a tour. Here are some phrases that may come in handy:

- ✔ **Lǚxíngshè zài nǎr?** (*lyew sheeng shuh dzye nar;* Where's the travel agency?)

- ✔ **Yǒu méiyǒu shuō Yīngwén de dǎoyóu?** (*yo mayo shwaw eeng one duh daow yo;* Are there any English-speaking guides?)

✔ **Bàn tiān duōshǎo qián?** (*bahn tyan dwaw shaow chyan;* How much for half a day?)

✔ **Nǐ yǒu méiyǒu lǚyóu shǒucè?** (*nee yo mayo lyew yo show tsuh;* Do you have a guidebook?)

✔ **Qǐngwèn, zài nǎr kéyǐ mǎi piào?** (*cheeng one, dzye nar kuh yee my pyaow;* Excuse me, where can I buy tickets for admission?)

✔ **Hǎo jíle. Piàojià duōshǎo?** (*how jee luh. pyaow jyah dwaw shaow;* Great. How much is the ticket price?)

✔ **Xiǎoháizi miǎnfèi ma?** (*shyaow hi dzuh myan fay mah;* Do children get in free?)

✔ **Wǒmen kě bù kéyǐ zhàoxiàng?** (*waw mun kuh boo kuh yee jaow shyahng;* May we take pictures?)

Going to the movies

So you want to relax, kick back, and take in a movie. What kind of movie do you want to see? Table 7-1 gives you a few genres to choose from:

Table 7-1	Movie Genres	
Chinese Word(s)	*Pronunciation*	*English Word(s)*
xǐjù piān	she jyew pyan	comedy
gùshi piān	goo shir pyan	drama
àiqíng piān	eye cheeng pyan	romance
dòngzuò piān	doong dzwaw pyan	action
jìlù piān	jee loo pyan	documentary
dònghuà piān	doong hwah pyan	cartoon
kǒngbù piān	koong boo pyan	horror
wǔxiá piān	woo shyah pyan	kung fu

Use the following conversation as an example of talking about movies:

Wendy: **Wǒmen jīntiān wǎnshàng qù kàn yíbù diànyǐng ba.** (*waw mun jin tyan wahn shahng chyew kahn ee boo dyan yeeng bah;* Let's go see a movie tonight.)

Tom: **Jīntiān yǎn shénme?** (*jin tyan yan shum-muh;* What's playing today?)

Wendy: **Yíge Zhāng Yìmóu dǎoyǎn de piānzi. Wǒ wàngle nèige míngzi.** (*ee guh jahng ee moe daow yan duh pyan dzuh. waw wahng luh nay guh meeng dzuh;* A film directed by Zhang Yimou. I forget the name.)

Tom: **Shì shuō Yīngwén de ma?** (*shir shwaw eeng one duh mah;* Is it in English?)

Wendy: **Búshì, kěshì yǒu Yīngwén zìmù.** (*boo shir, kuh shir yo eeng one dzuh moo;* No, but there are English subtitles.)

Words to Know

dǎoyǎn	daow yan	director
diànyǐng yuàn	dyan yeeng ywan	movie theater
Diànyǐng yuàn zài nǎr?	dyan yeeng ywan dzye nar	Where's the movie theater?
nán yǎnyuán	nahn yan ywan	actor
nǚ yǎnyuán	nyew yan ywan	actress
wàiguópiān	wye gwaw pyan	foreign film
Yīngwén zìmù	eeng one dzuh moo	English subtitles

Listening to a concert

You often hear that the language of music crosses international boundaries. If you're feeling a bit exhausted after practicing Chinese, you can head to a concert in the evening where you can relax. Let the music transport you to another mental space.

At the end of a concert in China, you don't hear anyone yelling "Encore!" What you do hear, however, is "**Zài lái yíge, zài lái yíge!**" (*dzye lye ee guh, dzye lye ee guh;* Bring on one more!)

Here are some words that may come in handy:

- **dàiwèiyuán** (*dye way ywan;* usher)
- **gē chàng huì** (*guh chahng hway;* choral recital)
- **gǔdiǎn yǐnyuè** (*goo dyan een yweh;* classical music)
- **jiāoxiǎng yuè** (*jyaow shyahng yweh;* symphonic music)
- **jiémùdān** (*jyeh moo dahn;* program)
- **juéshì yǐnyuè** (*jyweh shir een yweh;* jazz music)
- **míngē** (*meen guh;* folk song)
- **qì yuè** (*chee yweh;* instrumental music)
- **shìnèi yuè** (*shir nay yweh;* chamber music)
- **yáogǔn yuè** (*yaow gun yweh;* rock 'n' roll)
- **yǐnyuè huì** (*een yweh hway;* concert)
- **Zhōngguó gǔdiǎnyǐnyuè** (*joong gwaw goo dyan yeen yweh;* classical Chinese music)

Hopping around bars and clubs

The following phrases may come in handy when you're out exploring the local pubs and dance halls:

- **Qǐng lái yìpíng píjiǔ.** (*cheeng lye ee peeng pee jyo;* Please bring me a bottle of beer.)

✔ **Nǐ xiǎng gēn wǒ tiàowǔ ma?** (*nee shyahng gun waw tyaow woo mah;* Would you like to dance?)

✔ **Wǒ néng bùnéng qǐng nǐ hē jiǔ?** (*waw nung boo nung cheeng nee huh jyo;* May I get you a drink?)

✔ **Wǒmen dào nǎr qù tiàowǔ?** (*waw mun daow nar chyew tyaow woo;* Where can we go to dance?)

✔ **Yǒu méiyǒu rùchǎng fèi?** (*yo mayo roo chahng fay;* Is there a cover charge?)

When you go to a bar with friends, you may ask for some **bīngzhèn píjiǔ** (*beeng juhn pee jyo;* cold beer) or maybe some **hóng** (*hoong;* red) or **bái** (*bye;* white) **pútáo jiǔ** (*poo taow jyo;* wine). And don't forget to ask for some **huāshēngmǐ** (*hwah shung mee;* peanuts) or **tǔdòupiàn** (*too doe pyan;* potato chips) so you don't get too sloshed with all that **píjiǔ.**

Naming Your Hobbies

Having at least one **yèyú àihào** (*yeh yew eye how;* hobby) is always good. How about getting involved in some of the following?

✔ **diàoyú** (*dyaow yew;* fishing)

✔ **guójì xiàngqí** (*gwaw jee shyahng chee;* chess)

✔ **kàn shū** (*kahn shoo;* reading)

✔ **niǎo** (*nyaow;* birds)

✔ **pēngtiáo** (*pung tyaow;* cooking)

✔ **pīngpāngqiú** (*peeng pahng chyo;* Ping Pong)

✔ **pú kè** (*poo kuh;* cards)

✔ **tàijíquán** (*tye jee chwan;* commonly referred to just as *Tai Ji,* a slow form of martial arts)

✔ **yóupiào** (*yo pyaow;* stamps)

✔ **yuányì** (*ywan ee;* gardening)

If you want to ask a person what his or her hobby is, use the following terms.

> ✔ **Nǐ huì búhuì dǎ tàijíquán?** (*nee hway boo hway dah tiye jee chwahn;* Do you know how to do Tai Ji?)

> ✔ **Nǐ dǎ bùdǎ pīngpāngqiú?** (*nee dah boo dah peeng pahng chyo;* Do you play Ping Pong?)

> ✔ **Nǐ dǎ májiàng ma?** (*nee dah mah jyahng mah;* Do you play mah-jongg?)

Both **tàijíquán** and **májiàng** are quintessential Chinese pastimes. In addition to **tàijíquán,** everyone is familiar with other forms of **wǔshù** (*woo shoo;* martial arts), including kung fu — a martial art practiced since the Tang (*tahng*) dynasty back in the eighth century. In fact, you can still see kung fu masters practicing at the Shaolin Temple in Zhengzhou, Henan Province — one great reason for making a trip off the beaten path if you ever visit China.

Exploring Nature

If you want to get far from the madding crowds, or even just far enough away from your **bàngōngshì** (*bahn goong shir;* office) to feel refreshed, try going to one of the seven sacred **shān** (*shahn;* mountains) or a beautiful **hǎitān** (*hi tahn;* beach) to take in the **shānshuǐ** (*shahn shway;* scenery).

Here are some things you would see along the way if you were to travel through the Chinese countryside:

> ✔ **bǎotǎ** (*baow tah;* pagoda)

> ✔ **dàomiào** (*daow meow;* Daoist temple)

> ✔ **dàotián** (*daow tyan;* rice paddies)

> ✔ **fómiào** (*faw meow;* Buddhist temple)

> ✔ **kǒngmiào** (*koong meow;* Confucian temple)

> ✔ **miào** (*meow;* temple)

> ✔ **nóngmín** (*noong meen;* farmers)

If you're ever exploring **dàzìrán** (*dah dzuh rahn;* nature) with a friend who speaks Chinese, a few of these words may come in handy:

- ✔ **àn** (*ahn;* shore)
- ✔ **chítáng** (*chir tahng;* pond)
- ✔ **hǎi** (*hi;* ocean)
- ✔ **hǎitān** (*hi tahn;* beach)
- ✔ **hé** (*huh;* river)
- ✔ **hú** (*hoo;* lake)
- ✔ **shāmò** (*shah maw;* desert)
- ✔ **shān** (*shahn;* mountains)
- ✔ **shāndòng** (*shahn doong;* cave)
- ✔ **xiǎo shān** (*shyaow shahn;* hills)

Words to Know

fēngjǐng	fung jeeng	scenery
piàoliàng	pyaow lyahng	beautiful
tiāntáng	tyan tahng	paradise

To indicate a similarity between two ideas or objects, use the phrase **xiàng . . . yíyàng.** Here are some examples:

- ✔ **xiàng nǐ dìdi yíyàng** (*shyahng nee dee dee ee yahng;* like your younger brother)
- ✔ **xiàng qīngwā yíyàng** (*shyahng cheeng wah ee yahng;* like a frog)
- ✔ **xiàng fēngzi yíyàng** (*shyahng fungdzuh ee yahng;* like a crazy person)

Tapping into Your Artistic Side

Okay, now you're ready to tap into your more sensitive, artistic side in Chinese. Don't be afraid of expressing your **gǎnqíng** (*gahn cheeng;* emotions). The Chinese appreciate sensitivity to their Song (*soong*) dynasty **shānshuǐ huà** (*shahn shway hwah;* landscape painting) or the beauty of a Ming (*meeng*) dynasty **cíqì** (*tsuh chee;* porcelain).

I bet you have tons of **chuàngzàoxìng** (*chwahng dzaow sheeng;* creativity). If so, try your hand at one of these fine arts:

- ✔ **diāokè** (*dyaow kuh;* sculpting)
- ✔ **huà** (*hwah;* painting)
- ✔ **shūfǎ** (*shoo fah;* calligraphy)
- ✔ **shuǐcǎihuà** (*shway tsye hwah;* watercolor)
- ✔ **sùmiáohuà** (*soo meow hwah;* drawing)
- ✔ **táoqì** (*taow chee;* pottery)

Like kids all over the world, many Chinese children take **xiǎo tíqín** (*shyaow tee cheen;* violin) and **gāngqín** (*gahng cheen;* piano) classes — often under duress. Do you play a **yuè qì** (*yweh chee;* musical instrument)? How about trying your hand (or mouth) at one of these?

- ✔ **chángdí** (*chahng dee;* flute)
- ✔ **chánghào** (*chahng how;* trombone)
- ✔ **dà hào** (*dah how;* tuba)
- ✔ **dānhuángguǎn** (*dahn hwahng gwan;* clarinet)
- ✔ **dà tíqín** (*dah tee cheen;* cello)
- ✔ **gāngqín** (*gahng cheen;* piano)
- ✔ **gǔ** (*goo;* drums)
- ✔ **lǎba** (*lah bah;* trumpet)
- ✔ **jíta** (*gee tah;* guitar)
- ✔ **nán dǐyǐn** (*nahn dee een;* double bass)

✔ **sākèsīguǎn** (*sah kuh suh gwahn;* saxophone)

✔ **shuānghuángguǎn** (*shwahng hwahng gwan;* oboe)

✔ **shùqín** (*shoo cheen;* harp)

✔ **xiǎo tíqín** (*shyaow tee cheen;* violin)

✔ **zhōng tíqín** (*joong tee cheen;* viola)

If you've heard any traditional Chinese music at a concert or on a CD, you've probably heard one of these Chinese **yuè qì** (*yweh chee;* musical instruments) at one point or another:

✔ **èrhú** (*are hoo;* a two-stringed bowed instrument)

✔ **gǔzhēng** (*goo juhng;* a long, plucked string instrument that rests on a large stand in front of you)

✔ **pípa** (*pee pah;* a plucked string instrument with a fretted fingerboard that sits on your lap)

The Chinese language has a couple of different verbs that you can use to indicate the practice of various instruments.

✔ **For stringed instruments:** Use the verb **lā** (*lah;* to draw, as in draw a bow). For example, **lā zhōng tíqín** (*lah joong tee cheen;* play the viola).

✔ **For wind instruments:** Use **chuī** (*chway;* to blow).

✔ **For other instruments:** Use **tán** (*tahn;* play) a **gāngqín** (*gahng cheen;* piano).

Getting into Sports

No matter where you go in the world, you'll find a national pastime. In the United States, it's **bàngqiú** (*bahng chyo;* baseball). In most of Europe, it's **zúqiú** (*dzoo chyo;* soccer). And in China, it's **pīngpāngqiú** (*peeng pahng chyo;* Ping Pong). The following are popular sports you may encounter.

- **bàngqiú** (*bahng chyo;* baseball)

- **bīngqiú** (*beeng chyo;* hockey)

- **yīngshì zúqiú** (*eeng shir dzoo chyo;* soccer (*literally:* English-style football))

- **lánqiú** (*lahn chyo;* basketball)

- **lěiqiú** (*lay chyo;* softball)

- **páiqiú** (*pye chyo;* volleyball)

- **pīngpāngqiú** (*peeng pahng chyo;* Ping Pong)

- **shǒuqiú** (*show chyo;* handball)

- **tǐcāo** (*tee tsaow;* gymnastics)

- **wǎngqiú** (*wahng chyo;* tennis)

- **yǔmáoqiú** (*yew maow chyo;* badminton)

- **zúqiú** (*dzoo chyo;* football)

Yóuyǒng (*yo yoong;* swimming) is also a quite popular sport. Here are some related words:

- **cè yǒng** (*tsuh yoong;* side stroke)

- **dié yǒng** (*dyeh yoong;* butterfly stroke)

- **wā yǒng** (*wah yoong;* breast stroke or frog-style)

- **yǎng yǒng** (*yahng yoong;* backstroke)

- **yóuyǒng mào** (*yo yoong maow;* swimming cap)

- **zìyóu yǒng** (*dzuh yo yoong;* freestyle swimming)

Some games require the use of **pīngpāngqiú pāi** (*peeng pahng chyo pye;* Ping-Pong paddles); others require **wǎngqiú pāi** (*wahng chyo pye;* tennis rackets) or **lánqiú** (*lahn chyo;* basketballs). All games, however, require a sense of **gōngpíng jìngzhēng** (*goong peeng jeeng jung;* fair play).

Here are some useful phrases to know, whether you're an amateur or a professional athlete:

- **Wǒ xiǎng qù kàn qiúsài.** (*waw shyahng chyew kahn chyo sye;* I want to see a ballgame.)

- **Bǐsài shénme shíhòu kāishǐ?** (*bee sye shummuh shir ho kye shir;* When does the game begin?)

✔ **Bǐfēn duōshǎo?** (*bee fun dwaw shaow;* What's the score?)

✔ **Něixiē duì cānjiā bǐsài?** (*nay shyeh dway tsahn jya bee sye;* Which teams are playing?)

✔ **Wǒ yíngle.** (*waw yeeng luh;* I won.)

✔ **Nǐ shūle.** (*nee shoo luh;* You lost.)

✔ **Wǒ zhēn xūyào liànxí.** (*waw jun shyew yaow lyan she;* I really need to practice.)

✔ **méi tóuzhòng** (*may toe joong;* to miss the shot)

Here's a list of things that happen at sports events. You need to know these terms if you want to follow the action:

✔ **chuī shàozi** (*chway shaow dzuh;* to blow a whistle)

✔ **dǎngzhù qiú** (*dahng joo chyo;* to block the ball)

✔ **dé yì fēn** (*duh ee fun;* to score a point)

✔ **fā qiú** (*fah chyo;* to serve the ball)

✔ **méi tóuzhòng** (*may toe joong;* to miss the shot)

✔ **tījìn yì qiú** (*tee jeen ee chyo;* to make a goal)

Words to Know

cáipànyuán	tsye pahn ywan	referee
duìfāng	dway fahng	the opposing team
fànguī	fahn gway	foul
fēnshù	fun shoo	the score
jìfēnbǎn	jee fun bahn	scoreboard
píngjú	peeng jyew	tied

continued

Words to Know (continued)

shàngbànchǎng	shahng bahn chahng	first half of a game
tǐyù chǎng	tee yew chahng	stadium
xiàbànchǎng	shyah bahn chahng	second half of a game
zúqiú chǎng	dzoo chyo chahng	soccer field

Chapter 8

When You Gotta Work

• •

In This Chapter

▶ Managing the telephone

▶ Working around the office

▶ Using the Internet

• •

Dealing with the phone, making appointments, and sending letters and e-mails are all in a day's work. This chapter helps you get through your work-day in Chinese.

Picking Up a Telephone

This section gives you all the phrases you need to use the phone, to call friends as well as work, and to leave messages.

Telephone basics

Before even going near a **diànhuà** (*dyan hwah;* telephone), you may want to become familiar with some common Chinese words and phrases connected to using one.

▶ **běnshì diànhuà** (*bun shir dyan hwah;* local call)

▶ **chángtú diànhuà** (*chahng too dyan hwah;* long-distance call)

▶ **diànhuà hàomǎ** (*dyan hwah how mah;* telephone number)

- **diànhuàkǎ** (*dyan hwah kah;* phone card)
- **duìfāng fùfèi diànhuà** (*dway fahng foo fay dyan hwah;* collect call)
- **gōngyòng diànhuà** (*goong yoong dyan hwah;* public telephone)
- **guójì diànhuà** (*gwaw jee dyan hwah;* international phone calls)
- **jiēxiànyuán** (*jyeh shyan ywan;* operator)
- **shǒujī** (*show jee;* cell phone)
- **wúxiàn diànhuà** (*woo shyan dyan hwah;* cordless phone)

Here are some things you can do before, during, or after your call:

- **chá diànhuà hàomǎbù** (*chah dyan hwah how mah boo;* look a number up in a phonebook)
- **dǎ diànhuà** (*dah dyan hwah;* to make a phone call)
- **jiē diànhuà** (*jyeh dyan hwah;* answer a phone call)
- **guà diànhuà** (*gwah dyan hwah;* hang up)
- **huí diànhuà** (*hway dyan hwah;* return a phone call)
- **liú yíge huà** (*lyo ee guh hwah;* leave a message)
- **náqǐ diànhuà** (*nah chee dyan hwah;* pick up the phone)
- **shōudào diànhuà** (*show daow dyan hwah;* receive a phone call)

If you're like me, you need to ask plenty of basic questions before you figure out what you're doing with a telephone overseas. These questions may come in handy:

- **Zěnme dǎ diànhuà?** (*dzummuh dah dyan hwah;* How can I place a phone call?)
- **Zài nǎr kéyǐ dǎ diànhuà?** (*dzye nar kuh yee dah dyan hwah;* Where can I make a call?)

✔ **Běnshì diànhuà shōufèi duōshǎo qián?** (*bun shir dyan hwah show fay dwaw shaow chyan;* How much is a local phone call?)

The following words may come in handy now that most people use cell phones and beepers:

✔ **hū** (*who;* beep)

✔ **hūjī** (*who jee;* beeper)

✔ **hūjī hàomǎ** (*who jee how mah;* beeper number)

✔ **shǒujī** (*show jee;* cell phone)

✔ **shǒujī hàomǎ** (*show jee how mah;* cell phone number)

Here are some problems you may encounter while trying to make a phone call:

✔ **děnghòu** (*dung ho;* be on hold)

✔ **diànhuà huàile** (*dyan hwah hwye luh;* the phone is broken)

✔ **méi rén jiē diànhuà** (*may run jyeh dyan hwah;* no one answers)

✔ **méiyǒu bōhàoyīn** (*mayo baw how yeen;* no dial tone)

✔ **nǐ bōcuò hàomǎle** (*nee baw tswaw how mah luh;* you dialed the wrong number)

✔ **záyīn** (*dzah yeen;* static)

✔ **zhànxiàn** (*jahn shyan;* the line is busy)

Making a phone call

"**Wéi?**" (*way;* hello). You hear this word spoken in the second (or rising) tone a lot on the other end of the line when you make a phone call. It's kind of like testing the waters to see if someone is there. You can reply with the same word in the fourth (or falling) tone so it sounds like you're making a statement, or you can just get right to asking if the person you want to speak with is in at the moment. (For more about the four tones, see Chapter 1.)

A phrase you may hear on the other end of the line in mainland China is **"Nǐ nǎr?"** (*nee nar; literally:* where are you?). It asks what **dānwèi** (*dahn way;* work unit) you're attached to. After these first little questions, you may finally be ready to ask for the person you intended to call in the first place.

For decades after Communist rule took over mainland China in 1949, all Chinese people were assigned a **dānwèi**, which pretty much regulated every aspect of one's life — from where one lived, when one married, and even when one had children. Asking about one's **dānwèi** is still pretty common when answering the phone.

Here's how you might call to talk to a friend:

Mr. Chéng: **Wéi?** (*way;* Hello?)

Margaret: **Qǐngwèn, Luò Chéng zài ma?** (*cheeng one, law chung dzye mah;* May I please speak to Luo Cheng?)

Mr. Chéng: **Qǐngwèn, nín shì nǎ yí wèi?** (*cheeng one, neen shir nah ee way;* May I ask who's calling?)

Margaret: **Wǒ shì tāde tóngxué, Margaret.** (*waw shir tah duh toong shweh, Margaret;* I'm his classmate, Margaret.)

Mr. Chéng: **Hǎo. Shāoděng. Wǒ qù jiào tā.** (*how. shaow dung. waw chyew jyao tah;* Okay. Just a moment. I'll go get him.)

Calling places of business may be a bit different than the more informal call to a friend or coworker. When you call a **lyǔguǎn** (*lyew gwahn;* hotel), **shāngdiàn** (*shahng dyan;* store), or a particular **gōngsī** (*goong suh;* company), you may be asked what **fēnjī hàomǎ** (*fun jee how mah;* extension) you want. If you don't know, you can ask for the same:

Qǐngwèn, fēnjī hàomǎ shì duōshǎo? (*cheeng one, fun jee how mah shir dwaw shaow;* May I ask what the extension number is?)

After you figure out the extension, the **jiēxiànshēng** (*jyeh shyan shung;* operator) may say

Wǒ xiànzài jiù gěi nǐ jiē hào. (*waw shyan dzye jyo gay nee jyeh how;* I'll transfer you now.)

If you finally do get through to an employee's office only to discover the person isn't there, you can always leave a **yǒu shēng yóujiàn** (*yo shung yo jyan;* voicemail). When dealing with voicemail, you may have to deal with the following kinds of instructions on a recorded message:

✔ **Nín rúguǒ shǐyòng ànjiàn shì diànhuàjī, qǐng àn 3.** (*neen roo gwaw shir yoong ahn jyan shir dyan hwah jee, cheeng ahn sahn;* If you have a touch-tone phone, please press 3 now.)

✔ **Nín rúguǒ shǐyòng xuánzhuǎn bōhào jī, qǐng bié guà.** (*neen roo gwaw shir yoong shwan jwan baw how jee, cheeng byeh gwah;* If you have a rotary phone, please stay on the line.)

✔ **Yào huí dào zhǔ mùlù qǐng àn jǐngzìhào.** (*yow hway dow joo moo loo cheeng ahn jeeng dzuh how;* If you want to return to the main menu, please press # [pound] now.)

If you want to reach your **kèhù** (*kuh hoo;* client) or your **hégǔrén** (*huh goo run;* business partner) in today's business world, you may want some help from the **mìshū** (*mee shoo;* secretary) to connect you to the person you want to reach:

Jacob: **Liú Xiǎojiě, zěnme jiē wàixiàn?** (*lyo shyaow jyeh, dzummuh jyeh wye shyan;* Miss Liu, how can I get an outside line?)

Liú Xiǎojiě: **Méi wèntí. Wǒ bāng nǐ dǎ zhèige hàomǎ.** (*may one tee. waw bahng nee dah jay guh how mah;* Don't worry. I'll help you dial the number.)

Jacob: **Xièxiè.** (*shyeh shyeh;* Thanks.)

Liú Xiǎojiě: **Wéi? Zhè shì Wáng Xiānshēng de bàngōngshì ma?** (*way? jay shir wahng shyan* *shung duh bahn goong shir ma;* Hello? Do I have the office of Mr. Wang?)

Secretary: **Duìle. Jiù shì.** (*dway luh. jyoe shir;* Yes it is.)

Liú Xiǎojiē: **Kéyǐ gěi wǒ jiē tā ma?** (*kuh yee gay waw jyeh tah mah;* Can you connect me with him please?)

Secretary: **Duìbùqǐ, tā xiànzài kāihuì. Nǐ yào liúyán ma?** (*dway boo chee, tah shyan dzye kye hway. nee yaow lyo yan mah;* I'm sorry, he's in a meeting at the moment. Would you like to leave a message?)

Liú Xiǎojiē: **Máfan nǐ gàosù tā ABC gōngsī de jīnglǐ Jacob Smith gěi tā dǎ diànhuà le?** (*mah fahn nee gaow soo tah ABC goong suh duh jeeng lee Jacob Smith gay tah dah dyan hwah luh;* May I trouble you to tell him that Jacob Smith, the Manager of ABC Company, called him?)

Words to Know

fù zǒngcái	foo dzoong tsye	vice president
jīnglǐ	jeeng lee	manager
Qǐngwèn, nín shì nǎ yí wèi?	cheeng one, neen shir nah ee way	May I ask who's calling?
shāoděng	shaow dung	just a moment
wàixiàn	wye shyan	outside line
Wéi?	way	Hello?
Wèi.	way	Hello.
zhǔrèn	joo run	director
zǒngcái	dzoong tsye	president

Checking the answering machine

Because people lead such busy lives, you often have to **liúhuà** (*lyo hwah;* leave a message) on the **lùyīn diànhuà** (*loo yeen dyan hwah;* answering machine).

Here are some common greetings you may hear if you reach an answering machine:

- ✔ **Zhè shì Barry Jones.** (*jay shir Barry Jones;* You have reached Barry Jones.)

- ✔ **Wǒ xiànzài búzài.** (*waw shyan dzye boo dzye;* I'm not in at the moment/I'm away from my desk.)

- ✔ **Sān yuè sì hào zhīqián wǒ zài dùjià.** (*sahn yweh suh how jir chyan waw dzye doo jyah;* I'm on vacation until March 4th.)

- ✔ **Nín rúguǒ xiǎng gēn wǒde zhùshǒu tōnghuà, qǐng bō fēnjī 108.** (*neen roo gwaw shyahng gun waw duh joo show toong hwah, cheeng baw fun jee yaow leeng bah;* If you'd like to speak with my assistant, please dial extension 108.)

- ✔ **Qǐng liú xià nínde míngzi, diànhuà hàomǎ hé jiǎnduǎn de liúyán. Wǒ huì gěi nín huí diànhuà.** (*cheeng lyo shyah neen duh meeng dzuh, dyan hwah how mah huh jyan dwahn duh lyo yan. waw hway gay neen hway dyan hwah;* Please leave your name, number, and a brief message. I'll get back to you.)

When you leave a message on an answering machine, be sure to leave clear instructions about what you want the person to do:

- ✔ **Wǒ zài dǎ diànhuà gěi nǐ** (*waw dzye dah dyan hwah gay nee;* I'll call you again.)

- ✔ **Nǐ huí jiā zhīhòu qǐng dǎ diànhuà gěi wǒ.** (*nee hway jyah jir ho cheeng dah dyan hwah gay waw;* After you get home, please give me a call.)

- ✔ **Bié wàngle huí wǒde diànhuà.** (*byeh wahng luh hway waw duh dyan hwah;* Don't forget to return my call.)

If a live person answers and you have to leave a message, be polite. Keep these phrases in mind:

- **Qǐng gàosù tā wǒ gěi tā dǎ diànhuà le.** (*cheeng gaow soo tah waw gay tah dah dyan hwah luh;* Please tell her I called.*)

- **Máfan nǐ qǐng tā huí wǒde diànhuà.** (*mah fahn nee cheeng tah hway waw duh dyan hwah;* May I trouble you to please have him return my call?*)

- **Qǐng gàosù tā wǒ huì wǎn yìdiǎr lái.** (*cheeng gaow soo tah waw hway wahn ee dyar lye;* Please let him know I'll be a little late.*)

- **Qǐng gěi wǒ zhuǎn tāde liúyánjī?** (*cheeng gay waw jwan tah duh lyo yan jee;* Could you please transfer me to his voicemail?*)

Heading Off to Work

Time to get down to **shāngyè** (*shahng yeh;* business). Your **shāngyè**, that is. Want to know how to manage that job in Jiangsu or how to deal with the head honcho in Harbin? This section shows you everything from making a business appointment to conducting a meeting to checking your e-mail on the fly.

Your office digs

Whether you're a **mìshū** (*mee shoo;* secretary) or the **zhǔxí** (*joo she;* chairman) of the board, the atmosphere and physical environment of your **bàngōngshì** (*bahn goong shir;* office) is important.

These days, just about any office you work in or visit has the following basic items:

- **chuánzhēn** (*chwan jun;* fax)
- **diànhuà** (*dyan hwah;* telephone)
- **diànnǎo** (*dyan now;* computer)
- **dǎyìnjī** (*dah een jee;* printer)
- **fùyìnjī** (*foo een jee;* copier)

Of course, you first may want to look for the **kāfēijī** (*kah fay jee;* coffee machine), especially in the morning. In fact, the one part of the day you may look forward to the most is your **xiūxi** (*shyo she;* coffee break).

As you look around your **xiǎogéjiān** (*shyaow guh jyan;* cubicle), I bet you can find all of these items:

- ✔ **bǐjìběn** (*bee jee bun;* notebook)
- ✔ **dǎng'àn** (*dahng ahn;* file)
- ✔ **dìngshūjī** (*deeng shoo jee;* stapler)
- ✔ **gāngbǐ** (*gahng bee;* pen)
- ✔ **huíwénzhēn** (*hway one jun;* paper clip)
- ✔ **qiānbǐ** (*chyan bee;* pencil)
- ✔ **jiāodài** (*jyaow dye;* scotch tape)
- ✔ **xiàngpíjǐn** (*shyahng pee jeen;* rubberband)

If you can't find some indispensable item just when you need it, you can always ask someone in the next **xiǎogéjiān.** The simplest way to ask is by using the phrase

Nǐ yǒu méiyǒu ____? (*nee yo mayo _____?* do you have any _____?)

Use that phrase as often as you like. Just make sure you can reciprocate whenever your **tóngshì** (*toong shir;* coworker) needs something as well.

- ✔ **Nǐ yǒu méiyǒu gāngbǐ?** (*nee yo mayo gahng bee;* Do you have a pen?)
- ✔ **Nǐ yǒu méiyǒu dìngshūjī?** (*nee yo mayo deeng shoo jee;* Do you have a stapler?)

Conducting a meeting

Congratulations! You've finally set up shop in your new office in Beijing and are all set to have your first business meeting on foreign soil. But just what is the **mùdì** (*moo dee;* purpose) of your **huìyì** (*hway ee;*

meeting)? Is it to **yǎnshì** (*yan shir;* give a presentation) about a new **chǎnpǐn** (*chahn peen;* product)? Is it to **tánpàn** (*tahn pahn;* negotiate) a **hétóng** (*huh toong;* contract)? How about for the purpose of **shòuxùn** (*show shewn;* training) — either you or your Chinese colleagues? Do you have a specific **yìchéng** (*ee chung;* agenda) in mind already? I hope so. You definitely don't want to look unprepared.

Scheduling and planning a meeting

You may be one of those people who needs to **ānpái huìyì yìchéng** (*ahn pye hway ee ee chung;* schedule a meeting) just to prepare for another meeting. The following list includes a few tasks you may need to do at such a preliminary meeting:

✔ **jiějué wèntí** (*jyeh jweh one tee;* solve problems)

✔ **tǎolùn wèntí** (*taow lewn one tee;* discuss problems)

✔ **tuánduì jiànshè** (*twan dway jyan shuh;* team building)

✔ **zhìdìng huìyì yìchéng** (*jir deeng hway ee ee chung;* set an agenda)

If you want to make sure everyone has a say in planning matters, these phrases can help:

✔ **Jack, nǐ hái yǒu shénme xūyào bǔchōng ma?** (*Jack, nee hi yo shummuh shyew yaow boo choong mah;* Jack, do you have anything else to add?)

✔ **Wǒmen xūyào duì zhèige xiàngmù biǎojué ma?** (*waw mun shyew yaow dway jay guh shyahng moo byaow jweh mah;* Do we need to vote on this item?)

✔ **Shéi hái yǒu shénme yìjiàn huòzhě wèntí?** (*shay hi yo shummuh ee jyan hwaw juh one tee;* Who still has any comments or questions?)

Starting the meeting

When you're ready to get a business meeting started, these phrases can be helpful.

- ✔ **Zǎoshàng hǎo.** (*dzaow shahng how;* Good morning.)

- ✔ **Huānyíng nín dào wǒmen de bàngōngshì.** (*hwahn eeng neen dqow waw mun duh bahn goong shir;* Welcome to our office.)

- ✔ **Zài kāihuì yǐqián, ràng wǒmen zuò zuò zìwǒ jièshào.** (*dzye kye hway ee chyan, rahng waw mun dzwaw dzwaw dzuh waw jyeh shaow;* Before the meeting begins, let's introduce ourselves.)

- ✔ **Wǒ xiǎng jièshào yíxià huìyì de cānjiāzhě.** (*waw shyahng jyeh shaow ee shyah hway ee duh tsahn jya juh;* I'd like to introduce the conference participants.)

- ✔ **Zánmen kāishǐ ba.** (*dzahn mun kye shir bah;* Let's begin.)

Always greet the person who holds the highest rank first, before saying hello to others. Hierarchy is important to the Chinese, so try to always be conscious of this or you may unintentionally cause someone to "lose face" by not acknowledging his or her importance in the overall scheme of things. In order to follow this protocol, you need to know people's titles:

- ✔ **chǎngzhǎng** (*chahng jahng;* factory director)

- ✔ **dǒngshì** (*doong shir;* director of the board)

- ✔ **fù zǒngcái** (*foo dzoong tsye;* vice president)

- ✔ **jīnglǐ** (*jeeng lee;* manager)

- ✔ **shǒuxí kuàijì** (*show she kwye jee;* chief financial officer)

- ✔ **zhǔrèn** (*joo run;* director of a department)

- ✔ **zhǔxí** (*joo she;* chairman)
- ✔ **zǒngcái** (*dzoong tsye;* president)
- ✔ **zǔzhǎng** (*dzoo jahng;* team leader)

In Chinese, last names always come first. When addressing someone with a title, always say the last name first, followed by the title. So if you know someone's name is Li Peijie (Li being the surname), and he is the company director, you would address him as **Lǐ Zhǔrèn** (*Lee joo run;* Director Li).

Making a presentation

When you need to give a presentation during the meeting, you may want to use these terms:

- ✔ **bǎnzi** (*bahn dzuh;* board) and **fěnbǐ** (*fun bee;* chalk)
- ✔ **biǎogé** (*byaow guh;* charts)
- ✔ **chātú** (*chah too;* illustrations)
- ✔ **huàbǎn** (*hwah bahn;* easel) and **cǎibǐ** (*tsye bee;* marker)
- ✔ **túbiāo** (*too byaow;* diagrams)
- ✔ **zīliào** (*dzuh lyaow;* handouts)

Planning to go hi-tech instead? In that case you might want one of these:

- ✔ **PowerPoint yǎnshì** (*PowerPoint yan shir;* PowerPoint presentation)
- ✔ **huàndēngjī** (*hwahn dung jee;* slide projector) and **píngmù** (*peeng moo;* screen)
- ✔ **tóu yǐng piàn** (*toe eeng pyan;* transparency)

If you plan on videotaping your presentation, you need a **lùxiàngjī** (*loo shyahng jee;* video recorder). If the room is pretty big, you may also want to use a **màikèfēng** (*my kuh fung;* microphone).

Ending the meeting

Here are some phrases that can come in handy at the meeting's conclusion:

- Gǎnxiè dàjiā jīntiān chūxí huìyì. (*gahn shyeh dah jyah jeen tyan choo she hway ee;* Thank you everyone for participating in today's meeting.)

- Wǒmen xūyào zài kāihuì tǎolùn zhè jiàn shìqíng ma? (*waw mun shyew yaow dzye kye hway taow lwun jay jyan shir cheeng mah;* Do we need another meeting to continue the discussion?)

- Zài líkāi zhǐqián, wǒmen bǎ xià cì huìyì de rìqī dìng xiàlái ba. (*dzye lee kye jir chyan, waw mun bah shyah tsuh hway ee duh ir chee deeng shyah lye bah;* Before we leave, let's confirm a date for the next meeting.)

Words to Know

bào biǎo	baow byaow	spreadsheet
huìyì	hway ee	meeting; conference
huìyì yìchéng	hway ee ee chung	conference agenda
mùdì	moo dee	purpose
ruǎnjiàn	rwahn jyan	software
zīliào	dzuh lyaow	material

Discussing Business and Industry

You're sure to find one or another of the industries listed in Table 8-1 represented in mainland China, Taiwan, or Hong Kong.

Table 8-1	Foreign Industries with Representation in China, Taiwan, and Hong Kong	
Chinese	**Pronunciation**	**English**
guǎnggào hé gōngguān	gwahng gaow huh goong gwan	advertising and public relations
qìchē	chee chuh	automotive
yínháng yú cáiwù	yeen hahng yew tsye woo	banking and finance
diànnǎo	dyan now	computers
jiànzào	jyan dzaow	construction
gōngchéng	goong chung	engineering
yúlè	yew luh	entertainment
shízhuāng	shir jwahng	fashion
bǎoxiǎn	baow shyan	insurance
xīnwén	sheen one	journalism
guǎnlǐ zīxún	gwahn lee dzuh shwun	management consulting
cǎikuǎng yú shíyóu	tsye kwahng yew shir yo	mining and petroleum
zhìyào	jir yaow	pharmaceuticals
chūbǎn	choo bahn	publishing
fángdìchǎn	fahng dee chahn	real estate
yùn huò	yewn hwaw	shipping

Using the Internet

These days you can reach your business partner in Beijing in a matter of seconds through **diànzǐ kōngjiān** (*dyan dzuh koong jyan;* cyberspace). With **shǒutí shì** (*show tee shir;* portable) computers and multiple **jiǎnsuǒ yǐnqín** (*jyan swaw yeen cheen;* search engines), you can **jiǎnsuǒ guójì wǎngluò** (*jyan swaw gwaw jee wahng lwaw;* search the Internet) and find just about anything.

You can use your computer and the Internet for the following tasks:

- ✔ **ānzhuāng tiáozhì jiětiáoqì** (*ahn jwahng tyaow jir jyeh tyaow chee;* install a modem)
- ✔ **chóngxīn kāijī** (*choong sheen kye jee;* reboot)
- ✔ **dǎkāi diànnǎo** (*dah kye dyan now;* turn on the computer)
- ✔ **guāndiào diànnǎo** (*gwahn dyaow dyan now;* turn off the computer)
- ✔ **jiànlì yíge zhànghù** (*jyan lee ee guh jahng hoo;* set up an account)
- ✔ **jìn rù** (*jeen roo;* log on)
- ✔ **tuì chū** (*tway choo;* log off)
- ✔ **xiàzǎi wénjiàn** (*shyah dzye one jyan;* download a file
- ✔ **xuǎnzé yìjiā wǎngshàng fúwù tígōng shāng** (*shwan dzuh ee jya wahng shahng foo woo tee goong shahng;* choose an Internet service provider)

These days your **diànzǐ yóuxiāng dìzhǐ** (*dyan dzuh yo shyahng dee jir;* e-mail address) is as important as your **míngzi** (*meeng dzuh;* name) and your **diànhuà hàomǎ** (*dyan hwah how mah;* phone number) when it comes to keeping in touch. Here are some things you can do with e-mail after you have your own account:

- ✔ **fā diànzǐ yóujiàn** (*fah dyan dzuh yo jyan;* send an e-mail)

✔ **sòng wénjiàn** (*soong one jyan;* send a file)

✔ **zhuǎnfā xìnxi** (*jwan fah sheen she;* forward a message)

✔ **bǎ wénjiàn fùjiā zài diànzǐ yóujiàn** (*bah one jyan foo jyah dzye dyan dzuh yo jyan;* attach a file to an e-mail)

Words to Know

fúwùqì	foo woo chee	server
guójì	gwaw jee	international
jìshù fúwù	jee shoo foo woo	technical support
léishè guāngdié	lay shuh gwahng dyeh	CD-ROM
liúlǎn	lyo lahn	browse
liúlǎnqì	lyo lahn chee	browser
mìmǎ	mee mah	password
shàngwǎng	shahng wahng	to go online
wǎngyè	wahng yeh	Web page
wǎngzhàn	wahng jahn	Web site
wǎngzhǐ	wahng jir	URL
yīntèwǎng	een tuh wahng	the Internet
yònghù xìngmíng	yoong hoo sheeng meeng	user name

Chapter 9

I Get Around: Transportation

This chapter helps you make your way around the **fēijīchǎng** (*fay jee chahng;* airport), survive the **hǎiguān** (*hi gwahn;* Customs) experience, and board different types of **jiāotōng** (*jyaow toong;* transportation) after you reach your destination. It also shows you how to ask the occasional bystander for directions or give them yourself.

On the Move: Types of Transportation

You need to be able to get around with your language skills. The following sections give you some basic phrases to get you on the move.

Catching a plane

Ready to **bànlǐ dēngjǐ shǒuxù** (*bahn lee duhng jee show shyew;* check in)? After lugging your bags around, you finally get to **tuōyùn** (*twaw yewn;* check) your **xíngli** (*sheeng lee;* luggage). You receive a **dēngjīpái** (*duhng jee pye;* boarding pass) at the check-in counter, at which point you're ready to make your way to the appropriate **chūkǒu** (*choo ko;* gate), taking only your **shǒutí xíngli** (*show tee sheeng lee;* carry-on luggage).

All sorts of questions may be running through your mind about now. Here are some basic phrases that may come in handy during check in:

- ✔ **Wǒ xiǎng yào kào guòdào de wèizi.** (*waw shyahng yaow cow gwaw daow duh way dzuh;* I'd like an aisle seat.)

- ✔ **Wǒ xiǎng yào kào chuāng de wèizi.** (*waw shyahng yaow cow chwahng duh way dzuh;* I'd like a window seat.)

- ✔ **Wǒ xiǎng tuōyùn xíngli.** (*waw shyahng twaw yewn sheeng lee;* I'd like to check my luggage.)

- ✔ **Fēijī jǐ diǎn qǐfēi?** (*fay jee jee dyan chee fay;* What time does it depart?)

- ✔ **Wǒde hángbān hàomǎ shì duōshǎo?** (*waw duh hahng bahn how mah shir dwaw shaow;* What's my flight number?)

- ✔ **Zài jǐ hào mén hòujǐ?** (*dzye jee how mun ho jee;* Which gate do we leave from?)

The following conversation can help you with phrases you may encounter when getting on a plane:

Zhíyuán: **Nín hǎo. Qǐng chūshì nínde jīpiào.** (*neen how. cheeng choo shir neen duh jee pyaow;* Hello. Your ticket, please.)

Gordon: **Jiù zài zhèr.** (*jyo dzye jar;* Here it is.)

Zhíyuán: **Nín shì bú shì qù Běijīng? Néng kànkàn nínde hùzhào ma?** (*neen shir boo shir* *chyew bay jeeng? nuhng kahn kahn neen duh hoo jaow mah;* Are you going to Beijing? May I see your passport?)

Zhíyuán:**Yǒu jǐ jiàn xíngli?** (*yo jee jyan sheeng lee;* How many suitcases do you have?)

Gordon: **Wǒ yǒu sānge xiāngzi.** (*waw yo sahn guh shyahng dzuh;* I have three suitcases.)

Zhíyuán: **Yǒu méiyǒu shǒutí xíngli?** (*yo mayo show tee sheeng lee;* Do you have any carry-on luggage?)

Gordon: **Wǒ zhǐ yǒu yíge gōngwénbāo.** (*waw jir yo ee guh goong one baow;* I have only one briefcase.)

Zhíyuán: **Hǎo. Nín yào kào guòdào de wèizi háishì yào kào chuāng de wèizi?** (*how. neen yow cow gwaw daow duh way dzuh hi shir yaow cow chwahng duh way dzuh;* Okay. Would you like an aisle or a window seat?)

Gordon: **Wǒ xiǎng yào kào guòdào de wèizi.** (*waw shyahng yaow cow gwaw daow duh way dzuh;* I'd like an aisle seat.)

Zhíyuán: **Hǎo. Zhèi shì nǐde dēngjīpái. Qù Běijīng de 108 cì bānjī, 19 pái, B zuò.** (*how. jay shir nee duh duhng jee pye. chyew bay jeeng duh ee bye leeng bah tsuh bahn jee, shir jyo pye, B dzwaw;* Fine. Here's your boarding pass. Flight #108 to Beijing, Row 19, Seat B.)

Zhíyuán: **Zhè shì nínde xíngli lǐngqǔdān. Dàole Běijīng yǐhòu kěyǐ lǐngqǔ nínde xíngli.** (*jay shir neen duh sheeng lee leeng chyew dahn. daow luh bay jeeng ee ho kuh yee leeng chyew neen duh sheeng lee;* Here are your luggage claim tags. After you arrive in Beijing, you can claim your luggage.)

Gordon: **Xièxiè.** (*shyeh shyeh;* Thanks.)

Zhíyuán: **Zhù nín yí lù píng ān.** (*joo neen ee loo peeng ahn;* Have a nice trip.)

Words to Know

dàodá	daow dah	arrivals
fàngjìn zuòwèi dǐxià	fahng jin dzwaw way dee shyah	fit under the seat
gōngwénbāo	goong one baow	briefcase
guójì	gwaw jee	international
guónèi	gwaw nay	domestic
hùzhào	hoo jaow	passport
lǐngqǔdān	leeng chyew dahn	luggage claim tag
mén or chūkǒu	mun or choo ko	gate
piào	pyaow	ticket
qiānzhèng	chyan juhng	visa
qǐfēi	chee fay	departures
shǒutí xíngli	show tee sheeng lee	carry-on luggage
tóudǐng shàngfāng de xínglicāng	toe deeng shahng fahng duh sheeng lee tsahng	overhead compartment
xíngli	sheeng lee	luggage

Okay! You're all set to board the plane. Are you lucky enough to sit in the **tóuděngcāng** (*toe duhng tsahng;* first-class) section, or do you have to sit in **jīngjìcāng** (*jeeng jee tsahng;* economy class) the whole time? Either way, here are some people you see get on the plane before you:

- ✔ **chéngwùyuán** (*chung woo ywan;* flight attendants)
- ✔ **jiàshǐyuán** (*jyah shih ywan;* pilot)
- ✔ **jīzǔ** (*jee dzoo;* crew)

And if you're like me, you get worried about some things as the plane begins to taxi down the runway:

- ✔ **qǐfēi** (*chee fay;* take off)
- ✔ **qìliú** (*chee lyo;* turbulence)
- ✔ **zhuólù** (*jwaw loo;* landing)

You may also hear the **chéngwùyuán** say the following instructions:

- ✔ **Jìjǐn nǐde ānquándài.** (*jee jin nee duh ahn chwan dye;* Fasten your seat belt.)
- ✔ **Bù zhǔn chōuyān.** (*boo jwun cho yan;* No smoking permitted.)
- ✔ **Bǎ zuòyǐ kàobèi fàngzhí.** (*bah dzwaw ee cow bay fahng jir;* Put your seat back to the upright position.)
- ✔ **Bǎ tuōpán cānzhuō shōu qǐlái.** (*bah twaw pahn tsahn jwaw show chee lye;* Put your tray table back.)
- ✔ **Rúguǒ kōngqì yālì yǒu biànhuà, yǎngqìzhào huì zìdòng luòxià.** (*roo gwaw koong chee yah lee yo byan hwah, yahng chee jaow hway dzuh doong lwaw shyah;* If there's any change in air pressure, the oxygen mask will automatically drop down.)

If you're not a nervous flyer, you'll probably spend all your time listening to **yīnyuè** (*een yweh;* music) through the **ěrjī** (*are jee;* headset), flipping **píndào** (*peen daow;* dials) on the radio or **diànshì tái** (*dyan* *shir tye;* channels) on the television, or trying to **shuìjiào** (*shway jyaow;* sleep). I hope the flight is showing a good **diànyǐng** (*dyan yeeng;* movie) on such a long trip.

If things are going a little slow, you may use these phrases:

- ✔ **Qǐng wèn, wǒmen de fēijī huì búhuì zhèngdiǎn qǐfēi?** (*cheeng one, waw mun duh fay jee hway boo hway juhng dyan chee fay;* Excuse me, but will our plane be departing on time?)
- ✔ **Hěn duìbùqǐ. Fēijī yào tuīchí chàbùduō bànge xiǎoshí.** (*hun dway boo chee. fay jee yaow tway chir chah boo dwaw bahn guh shyaow shir;* I'm very sorry. Takeoff has been postponed for about a half an hour.)

Words to Know

chàbùduō	chah boo dwaw	about; almost (approximately)
jǐnjí chūkǒu	jin jee choo ko	emergency exits
jiùshēngyī	jyo shung ee	life vests
zhèngdiǎn	juhng dyan	on time
zuǒyòu	dzwaw yo	approximately

Hailing a cab

Renting a car in China is virtually impossible, so take a taxi and relax. Let the driver worry about how to get you from point A to point B. Here's what you say to the hotel door attendant if you want help hailing a cab:

Wǒ yào jiào jīchéngchē. (*waw yaow jyaow jee chung chuh;* I would like a taxi.)

You can also say

> **Wǒ yào jiào chūzūchē.** (*waw yaow jyaow choo dzoo chuh;* I would like a taxi.)

The two methods are interchangeable, just like saying "taxi" or "cab."

After you're safely in the cab, you need to know how to say the following phrases:

- ✔ **Qǐng dài wǒ dào zhèige dìzhǐ.** (*cheeng dye waw daow jay guh dee jir;* Please take me to this address.)

- ✔ **Qǐng dǎ biǎo.** (*cheeng dah byaow;* Please turn on the meter.)

- ✔ **Qǐng kāi màn yìdiǎr.** (*cheeng kye mahn ee dyar;* Please drive a little slower.)

- ✔ **Qǐng kāi kuài yìdiǎr.** (*cheeng kye kwye ee dyar;* Please drive a little faster.)

- ✔ **Wǒ děi gǎn shíjiān.** (*waw day gahn shir jyan;* I'm in a hurry.)

- ✔ **Qǐng zǒu fēngjǐng hǎo de lù.** (*cheeng dzoe fung jeeng how duh loo;* Please take a scenic route.)

- ✔ **Zài zhèr guǎi wār.** (*dzye jar gwye wahr;* Turn here.)

- ✔ **Nǐ kéyǐ děng jǐ fēn zhōng ma?** (*nee kuh yee duhng jee fun joong mah;* Can you wait a few minutes?)

Oh, and one more thing. As you **chūfā** (*choo fah;* set off) with your taxi **sījī** (*suh jee;* driver), make sure you put on your **ānquándài** (*ahn chwan dye;* seat belt).

Finally, before you get out of the cab, these phrases may come in handy for price negotiations:

- ✔ **Wǒ gāi gěi nǐ duōshǎo qián?** (*waw guy gay nee dwaw shaow chyan;* How much do I owe you?)

- ✔ **Wǒ huì àn biǎo fù kuǎn.** (*waw hway ahn byaow foo kwahn;* I'll pay what the meter says.)

✔ **Bié qīpiàn wǒ.** (*byeh chee pyan waw;* Don't cheat me.)

✔ **Kāi wán xiào! Wǒ jùjué fù zhèmme duō qián.** (*kye wahn shyaow! waw jyew jweh foo juhmmah dwaw chyan;* You've got to be kidding! I refuse to pay so much.)

✔ **Bú yòng zhǎo le.** (*boo yoong jaow luh;* Keep the change.)

✔ **Qǐng gěi wǒ shōujù.** (*cheeng gay waw show jyew;* Please give me a receipt.)

Words to Know

chē	chuh	car
chéngkè	chuhng kuh	passenger
chūzūchē	choo dzoo chuh	taxi
dǔchē	doo chuh	traffic jam
gāofēngqī	gaow fung chee	rush hour
jìchéngbiǎo	jee chuhng byaow	meter
kāi chē	kye chuh	to drive a car
sījī	suh jee	driver
wènlù	one loo	to ask for directions
xiǎofèi	shyaow fay	tip

Hopping on the bus

Gōnggòng qìchē (*goong goong chee chuh;* buses) are almost as common as bicycles in China. They also cost much less than **chūzūchē** (*choo dzoo chuh;* taxis), but you'll need these phrases:

✔ **Yīnggāi zuò jǐ lù chē?** (*eeng guy dzwaw jee loo chuh;* Which (number) bus should I take?)

✔ **Yīnggāi zuò sān lù chē. Nèige gōnggòng qìchē zhàn jiù zài zhèr.** (*eeng guy dzwaw sahn loo chuh. nay guh goong goong chee chuh jahn jyo dzye jar;* You should take the number 3 bus. That bus stop is right here.)

✔ **Chē piào duōshǎo qián?** (*chuh pyaow dwaw shaow chyan;* How much is the fare?)

✔ **Gōnggòng qìchē zhàn zài nǎr?** (*goong goong chee chuh jahn dzye nar;* Where's the bus station?)

✔ **Duōjiǔ lái yítàng?** (*dwaw jyo lye ee tahng;* How often does it come?)

✔ **Qǐng gàosù wǒ zài nǎr xià chē.** (*cheeng gaow soo waw dzye nar shyah chuh;* Please let me know where to get off.)

Words to Know

gōnggòng qìchē	goong goong chee chuh	bus
gōnggòng qìchē zhàn	goong goong chee chuh jahn	bus station
hái hǎo	hi how	it's okay; not too bad
jǐ lù?	jee loo	which route?
jǐ lù chē?	jee loo chuh	which number bus?
yuè piào	yweh pyaow	monthly pass

Riding the rails

If you want to get where you need to go really quickly, especially in Hong Kong, the fastest way is the **dìtiě** (*dee tyeh;* subway). Hong Kong's **dìtiě zhàn** (*dee tyeh jahn;* subway stations) are pretty easy to navigate.

Unlike in Hong Kong, the subway system in mainland China is relatively new, and you only find stations in less than a handful of cities. Aboveground **huǒchē** (*hwaw chuh;* train) travel, however, is tried and true. You can find plenty of **huǒchēzhàn** (*hwaw chuh jahn;* train stations) in China. They even come equipped with **hòuchēshì** (*ho chuh shir;* waiting rooms).

If you plan to travel a long distance, be sure to book a **ruǎnwò** (*rwan waw;* soft sleeper) for such occasions — or at least ask for a **ruǎnzuò** (*rwan dzwaw;* soft seat). Table 9-1 gives you the goods on the types of seats in trains.

Table 9-1	Seating Accommodations on Trains	
Chinese Word	*Pronunciation*	*English Words*
yìngzuò	eeng dzwaw	hard seat
ruǎnzuò	rwan dzwaw	soft seat
yìngwò	eeng waw	hard sleeper
ruǎnwò	rwahn waw	soft sleeper
xiàpù	shyah poo	lower berth
shàngpù	shahng poo	upper berth

Before you **shàngchē** (*shahng chuh;* board the train), you need to go to the **shòupiàochù** (*show pyaow choo;* ticket office) to buy your **piào** (*pyaow;* ticket). You use the following words and phrases to get the job done:

- **dānchéngpiào** (*dahn chuhng pyaow;* one-way ticket)
- **láihuípiào** (*lye hway pyaow;* roundtrip ticket)
- **mànchē** (*mahn chuh;* local train)
- **piào** (*pyaow;* ticket)
- **piàojià** (*pyaow jyah;* fare)
- **shòupiàochù** (*show pyaow choo;* ticket office)
- **tèkuài** (*tuh kwye;* express train)

The following questions may come in handy at the train station:

- **Piàofáng zài nǎr?** (*pyaow fahng dzye nar;* Where's the ticket office?)

  Notice the different way of saying ticket office in this question. Options abound in the Chinese language.
- **Wǒ yào yìzhāng yìngwò piào.** (*waw yow ee jahng eeng waw pyaow;* I'd like a hard-sleeper ticket.)
- **Huǒchē cóng něige zhàntái kāi?** (*hwaw chuh tsoong nay guh jahn tye kye;* Which gate does the train leave from?)

And when you finally hear the **lièchēyuán** (*lyeh chuh ywan;* conductor) say **"Shàng chē le!"** (*shahng chuh luh;* All aboard!), you can board and ask the following questions:

- **Zhèige zuòwèi yǒu rén ma?** (*jay guh dzwaw way yo run mah;* Is this seat taken?)
- **Cānchē zài nǎr?** (*tsahn chuh dzye nar;* Where's the dining car?)

Words to Know

cānchē	tsahn chuh	dining car
chápiào	chah pyaow	check the ticket
huànchē	hwahn chuh	change trains
huí lái	hway lye	to return
lái huí piào	lye hway pyaow	roundtrip ticket
shíkèbiǎo	shir kuh byaow	time schedule
zhàntái	jahn tye	platform

Going through Customs

Surviving **hǎiguān** (*hi gwahn;* Customs) is an experience, especially if none of the **hǎiguān guānyuán** (*hi gwahn gwahn ywan;* Customs officers) **dǒng Yīngyǔ** (*doong eeng yew;* understand English). Table 9-2 lists the items you need to have ready at Customs. The following phrases can come in handy, too:

✔ **Nǐ dǒng Yīngyǔ ma?** (*nee doong eeng yew mah;* Do you understand English?)

✔ **Wǒ shì Měiguó rén.** (*waw shir may gwaw run;* I'm American.)

✔ **Wǒ shì Yīngguó rén.** (*waw shir eeng gwaw run;* I'm British.)

✔ **Wǒ shì Jiānádà rén.** (*waw shir jyah nah dah run;* I'm Canadian.)

✔ **Xīshǒujiān zài nǎr?** (*she show jyan dzye nar;* Where are the restrooms?)

Table 9-2   Items to Have Ready at Customs

Chinese Word(s)	Pronunciation	English Word(s)
rùjìng dēngjì kǎ	roo jeeng duhng jee kah	arrival card
chūjìng dēngjì kǎ	choo jeeng duhng jee kah	departure card
jiànkāng zhèng	jyan kahng juhng	health certificate
shēnbào de wùpǐn	shun baow duh woo peen	articles to declare
xiāngyān	shyahng yan	cigarettes
jiǔ	jyo	alcohol
bāo	baow	bag
xiāngzi	shyahng dzuh	suitcase
xíngli	sheeng lee	luggage

The **hǎiguān guānyuán** may ask you a couple of these important questions:

- ✔ **Nǐ yǒu méiyǒu yào shēnbào de wùpǐn?** (*nee yo mayo yaow shun baow duh woo peen;* Do you have anything you want to declare?)

- ✔ **Qǐng gěi wǒ kànkàn nǐde hùzhào.** (*cheeng gay waw kahn kahn nee duh hoo jaow;* Please show me your passport.)

- ✔ **Qǐng gěi wǒ kànkàn nǐde hǎiguān shēnbàodān.** (*cheeng gay waw kahn kahn nee duh hi gwan shun baow dahn;* Please show me your Customs declaration form.)

- ✔ **Nǐ dǎsuàn zài zhèr dāi duōjiǔ?** (*nee dah swan dzye jar dye dwaw jyo;* How long do you plan on staying?)

- ✔ **Nǐ lái zhèr shì bàn gōngwù háishì lǚyóu?** (*nee lye jar shir ban goong woo hi shir lyew yo;* Are you here on business or as a tourist?)

Customs agents aren't the only people with questions to ask. You may have some questions you want to try out yourself:

> ✔ **Xíngli yào dǎkāi ma?** (*sheeng lee yaow dah kye mah;* Should I open my luggage?)
>
> ✔ **Xíngli kéyǐ shōu qǐlái ma?** (*sheeng lee kuh yee show chee lye mah;* May I close my suitcases now?)
>
> ✔ **X guāng huì sǔnhuài wǒde jiāojuǎn ma?** (*X gwahng hway swuhn hwye waw duh jyaow jwan mah;* Will the X-ray damage my film?)
>
> ✔ **Wǒ yào fù shuì ma?** (*waw yaow foo shway mah;* Must I pay duty?)

Words to Know

gōngwù	goong woo	to be on business
jiāo shuì	jyaow shway	pay duty
lùguò	loo gwaw	passing through
lǚyóu	lyew yo	tour
qǔ xíngli chù	chyew sheeng lee choo	baggage-claim area

Asking for Directions

Everyone (yes, even you) has to ask for **fāngxiàng** (*fahng shyahng;* directions) at some time or another. This section helps you figure out exactly how to ask for directions before you ever **mílù** (*mee loo;* get lost).

Avoiding 20 questions:
Just ask "where"

The easiest way to ask where something is in Chinese is to use the question word **năr** (*nar*). It means "where." But you can't just say **năr,** or folks still won't know what you're talking about. You have to use the coverb **zài** (*dzye*) in front of **năr** (**zài năr**), which can be translated as "in" or "at." Just put the name of whatever you're looking for before the word **zài** to create a complete question:

- ✔ **Yóujú zài năr?** (*yo jyew dzye nar;* Where's the post office?)

- ✔ **Shūdiàn zài năr?** (*shoo dyan dzye nar;* Where's the bookstore?)

- ✔ **Nĭ zài năr?** (*nee dzye nar;* Where are you?)

Here are some more places you may be looking for when you lose your way:

- ✔ **cèsuŏ** (*tsuh swaw;* bathroom)

- ✔ **chūzū qìchēzhàn** (*choo dzoo chee chuh jahn;* taxi stand)

- ✔ **dìtiĕzhàn** (*dee tyeh jahn;* subway station)

- ✔ **fànguăn** (*fahn gwahn;* restaurant)

- ✔ **gōnggòngqìchēzhàn** (*goong goong chee chuh jahn;* bus stop)

- ✔ **huŏchēzhàn** (*hwaw chuh jahn;* train station)

- ✔ **jízhĕnshì** (*jee juhn shir;* emergency room)

- ✔ **Mĕiguó Dàshĭguăn** (*may gwaw dah shir gwahn;* American Embassy)

- ✔ **piàofáng** (*pyaow fahng;* ticket office)

- ✔ **xuéxiào** (*shweh shyaow;* school)

- ✔ **yínháng** (*een hahng;* bank)

When you travel in unknown areas, you may need to determine whether you can walk or if you need to take a **gōnggòng qìchē** (*goong goong chee chuh;* bus) or **chūzū qìchē** (*choo dzoo chee chuh;* taxi) to reach your destination:

▸ **Hěn jìn ma?** (*hun jeen mah;* Is it near?)

▸ **Hěn yuǎn ma?** (*hun ywan mah;* Is it far?)

The word **nǎr** spoken with a third (low falling and then rising) tone means "where," but the same word said with a fourth (falling) tone, **nàr**, means "there," so be particularly careful which tone you use when you ask for directions. The person you ask may think you're making a statement, not asking a question. (See Chapter 1 for more on tones.)

Words to Know

dìzhǐ	dee jir	address
fāngxiàng	fahng shyahng	directions
zuò chūzū qìchē	dzwaw choo dzoo chee chuh	to take a taxi
zuò gōnggòng qìchē	dzwaw goong goong chee chuh	to take the bus

Getting direction about directions

Knowing how to ask where you can find a particular place is the first step, but you also need to know how to get there. Here's the simplest way to find out:

Qù . . . . zěnme zǒu? (*chyew dzummuh dzoe;* How do I get to_____?)

Here are some examples of how to use this question pattern:

✔ **Qù fēijīchǎng zěnme zǒu?** (*chyew fay jee chahng dzummuh dzoe;* How do I get to the airport?)

✔ **Qù túshūguǎn zěnme zǒu?** (*chyew too shoo gwahn dzummuh dzoe;* How do I get to the library?)

✔ **Qù xuéxiào zěnme zǒu?** (*chyew shweh shyaow dzummuh dzoe;* How do I get to the school?)

Answering "where" questions

Short of using international sign language with a pantomime act, you may want to get a handle on some basic terms that indicate direction and location. Read on for a quick list:

✔ **yòu** (*yo;* right)

✔ **zuǒ** (*dzwaw;* left)

✔ **qián** (*chyan;* front)

✔ **hòu** (*ho;* back)

✔ **lǐ** (*lee;* inside)

✔ **wài** (*why;* outside)

✔ **shàng** (*shahng;* above)

✔ **xià** (*shyah;* below)

✔ **duìmiàn** (*dway myan;* opposite)

✔ **kàojìn** (*kaow jeen;* next to)

If you plan to indicate that something is inside, outside, above, below, in front of, or behind something else, you can use three different completely interchangeable word endings with any of the location words:

✔ **biàn** (*byan*)

✔ **miān** (*myan*)

✔ **tóu** (*toe*)

So, for example, if you want to say that the dog is outside, you can say it in any of the following ways:

- ✔ **Gŏu zài wàimiàn.** (*go dzye why myan;* The dog is outside.)
- ✔ **Gŏu zài wàibiān.** (*go dzye why byan;* The dog is outside.)
- ✔ **Gŏu zài wàitóu.** (*go dzye why toe;* The dog is outside.)

Words to Know

duì miàn	dway myan	opposite
kāi chē	kye chuh	to drive
shàng	shahng	to get on
wàng	wahng	toward
xià	shyah	to get off
zŏu (zŏu lù)	dzoe (dzoe loo)	to walk
zuò huŏchē	zwaw hwaw chuh	to take the train

Giving directions

Knowing how to give directions comes in handy when you think the taxi driver is about to take you for a ride (figuratively, that is) because he figures you don't know your way around town.

If you really do know your way around the city, you use the following words to instruct the taxi driver which way you want to go:

> ✔ **dìxiàdào** (*dee shyah daow;* underpass)
>
> ✔ **gāosùgōnglù** (*gaow soo goong loo;* freeway)
>
> ✔ **gōnglù** (*goong loo;* highway)
>
> ✔ **guǎijiǎo** (*gwye jyaow;* corner)
>
> ✔ **lù** (*loo;* road)
>
> ✔ **qiáo** (*chyaow;* bridge)
>
> ✔ **tiānqiáo** (*tyan chyaow;* overpass)
>
> ✔ **xiàngzi** (*shyahng dzuh;* alley or lane)

Wherever you want to go, you need to know a few key verbs to instruct the cab driver:

> ✔ **guò** (*gwaw;* to pass)
>
> ✔ **shàng** (*shahng;* to go up)
>
> ✔ **xià** (*shyah;* to go down)
>
> ✔ **yòu zhuǎn** (*yo jwan;* turn right)
>
> ✔ **zuǒ zhuǎn** (*dzwaw jwan;* turn left)
>
> ✔ **zhí zǒu** (*jir dzoe;* go straight ahead)
>
> ✔ **zhuǎn wān** (*jwan wahn;* turn around)

If you don't know an exact location, you can also convey less specific details:

> ✔ **fùjìn** (*foo jeen;* near)
>
> ✔ **sìzhōu** (*suh joe;* around)

Expressing distances with lí

To indicate the distance from one place to another, you need to use the "distance from" coverb "**lí**" (*lee*). The general sentence pattern looks something like this:

Place word + **lí** + place word + description of the distance

For example:

> ✔ **Gōngyuán lí túshūguǎn hěn jìn.** (*goong ywan lee too shoo gwan hun jeen;* The park is very close to the library.)

> ✔ **Wǒ jiā lí nǐ jiā tǐng yuǎn.** (*waw jyah lee nee jyah teeng ywan;* My home is really far from your home.)

If you want to specify exactly how far one place is from another, you use the number of **lǐ** (*lee;* the Chinese equivalent of a kilometer) followed by the word **lǐ** and then the word **lù** (*loo; literally:* road). Whether you say **sì lǐ lù** (*suh lee loo;* 4 kilometers), **bā lǐ lù** (*bah lee loo;* 8 kilometers), or **èrshísān lǐ lù** (*are shir sahn lee loo;* 23 kilometers), people know the exact distance when you use this pattern. You also have to use the word **yǒu** (*yo;* to have) before the number of kilometers. If the answer includes an adjectival verb such as **yuǎn** (*ywan;* far) or **jìn** (*jin;* close) rather than a numerical distance, however, you don't need to specify the number of kilometers or use the word **yǒu**.

Check out the following samples questions and answers that use these new patterns:

> ✔ **Gōngyuán lí túshūguǎn duōme yuǎn?** (*goong ywan lee too shoo gwahn dwaw mah ywan;* How far is the park from the library?)

> ✔ **Gōngyuán lí túshūguǎn yǒu bā lǐ lù.** (*goong ywan lee too shoo gwahn yo bah lee loo;* The park is eight kilometers from the library.)

> ✔ **Yínháng lí nǐ jiā duōme jìn?** (*een hahng lee nee jyah dwaw mah jin;* How close is the bank from your home?)

> ✔ **Hěn jìn. Zhǐ yì lǐ lù.** (*hun jin. jir ee lee loo;* Very close. Just one kilometer.)

You may have some other questions when you inquire about locations and distances:

- ✔ **Yào duō cháng shíjiān?** (*yaow dwaw chahng shir jyan;* How long will it take?)

- ✔ **Zǒu de dào ma?** (*dzoe duh daow mah;* Can I walk there?)

- ✔ **Zǒu de dào, zǒu bú dào?** (*dzoe duh daow, dzoe boo daow;* Can one walk there?)

Specifying cardinal points with directional coverbs

You can tell someone to go **yòu** (*yo;* right) or **zuǒ** (*dzwaw;* left) until you're blue in the face, but sometimes the best way to give people directions is to point them the right way with the cardinal points: north, south, east, or west.

In Chinese, however, you say them in this order:

- ✔ **běi** (*bay;* north)

- ✔ **dōng** (*doong;* east)

- ✔ **nán** (*nahn;* south)

- ✔ **xī** (*she;* west)

To give more precise directions, you may have to use the following:

- ✔ **dōng běi** (*doong bay;* northeast)

- ✔ **dōng nán** (*doong nahn;* southeast)

- ✔ **xī běi** (*she bay;* northwest)

- ✔ **xī nán** (*she nahn;* southwest)

When indicating north, south, east, west, left, or right, you use either **-biān** (*byan*) or **-miàn** (*myan*) as word endings, but not **-tóu** (*toe*), which you can use with other position words such as front, back, inside, and outside.

Giving directions often entails multiple instructions. You can't always say "make a right and you're there" or "go straight and you'll see it right in front of you." Sometimes you have to use a common Chinese pattern for giving multiple directions. That pattern is

xiān + Verb #1, **zài** + Verb #2

This translates into "first you do X, and then you do Y." Here are some examples:

- ✔ **Xiān wàng dōng zǒu, zài wàng yòu zhuǎn.** (*shyan wahng doong dzoe, dzye wahng yo jwan;* First walk east, and then turn right.)

- ✔ **Xiān zhí zǒu, zài wàng xǐ zǒu.** (*shyan jir dzoe, dzye wahng she dzoe;* First go straight, and then turn west.)

Here's an example conversation:

George: **Qǐng wèn. Shànghǎi bówùguǎn lí zhèr hěn yuǎn ma?** (*cheeng one. shahng hi baw woo gwahn lee jar hun ywan mah;* Excuse me. Is the Shanghai Museum very far from here?)

Stranger: **Bù yuǎn. Shànghǎi bówùguǎn jiù zài rénmín dà dào.** (*boo ywan. Shahng hi baw woo gwahn jyo dzye run meen dah daow;* It's not far at all. The Shanghai Museum is on the Avenue of the People.)

George: **Rénmín dà dào lí zhèr duōme yuǎn?** (*run meen dah daow lee jar dwaw mah ywan;* How far is the Avenue of the People from here?)

Stranger: **Rénmín dà dào lí zhèr zhǐ yǒu yǐ lǐ lù zuǒyòu.** (*run meen dah daow lee jar jir yo ee lee loo dzwaw yo;* The Avenue of the People is only about one kilometer from here.)

George: **Cóng zhèr zǒu de dào, zǒu bú dào?** (*tsoong jar dzoe duh daow, dzoe boo daow;* Can I walk there from here?)

Stranger: **Kěndìng zǒu de dào. Nǐ xiān wàng nán zǒu, zài dì èr tiáo lù wàng xǐ zhuǎn. Dì yǐ ge lóu jiù shì.** (*kun deeng dzoe duh daow. nee shyan wahng nahn dzoe, dzye dee are tyaow loo wahng she jwan. dee ee guh low jyoe shir;* It's certainly walkable. Walk north first, and then turn west at the second street. It'll be the first building you see.)

George: **Fēicháng gǎnxiè nǐ.** (*fay chahng gahn shyeh nee;* I'm extremely grateful (for your help).)

Stranger: **Méi shì.** (*may shir;* It's nothing.)

Chapter 10

Finding a Place to Lay Your Weary Head

● ●

In This Chapter

▶ Booking your room reservation

▶ Checking in upon arrival

▶ Requesting hotel service

▶ Packing your bags and paying your bill

● ●

he right **lǚguǎn** (*lyew gwahn;* hotel) can make or break a vacation. This chapter runs you through the gamut of booking your hotel, checking in at the front desk, checking out at the designated time, and dealing with all sorts of issues that may come up in between.

First, however, I have an astounding fact for you: You have not one, not two, but as many as five ways to say the word "hotel" in Chinese:

✔ **lǚguǎn** (*lyew gwahn;* hotel)

✔ **fàndiàn** (*fahn dyan; literally:* a place for meals)

✔ **jiǔdiàn** (*jyo dyan; literally:* a place for wine)

✔ **zhāodàisuǒ** (*jaow dye swaw; literally:* a place to receive people)

✔ **bīnguǎn** (*been gwahn; literally:* a place for guests)

Making a Room Reservation

Are you thinking of **yùdìng** (*yew deeng;* reserving) a hotel **fángjiān** (*fahng jyan;* room)? What kind do you want? A **dānrén fángjiān** (*dahn run fahng jyan;* single room) all for yourself? A **shuāngrén fángjiān** (*shwahng run fahng jyan;* double room) for you and your special someone? Or perhaps a penthouse **tàojiān** (*taow jyan;* suite) for a special occasion like your 50th wedding **zhōunián** (*joe nyan;* anniversary)?

Here are some questions you may want to ask over the phone as you begin the search for your **lǐxiǎng** (*lee shyahng;* ideal) hotel:

- ✔ **Nǐmen hái yǒu fángjiān ma?** (*nee mun hi yo fahng jyan mah;* Do you have any rooms available?)

- ✔ **Nǐmen fángjiān de jiàgé shì duōshǎo?** (*nee mun fahng jyan duh jyah guh shir dwaw shaow;* How much are your rooms?)

- ✔ **Nà shì dānrén fángjiān hái shì shuāngrén fángjiān de jiàgé?** (*nah shir dahn run fahng jyan hi shir shwahng run fahng jyan duh jyah guh;* Is that the price of a single room or a double?)

- ✔ **Nǐmen yào dāi jǐ ge wǎnshàng?** (*nee mun yaow dye jee guh wahn shahng;* How many nights will you be staying?)

- ✔ **Wǒ yào yíge fángjiān zhù liǎng ge wǎnshàng.** (*waw yaow ee guh fahng jyan joo lyahng guh wahn shahng;* I'd like a room for two nights.)

- ✔ **Nǐmen shōu bù shōu xìnyòng kǎ?** (*nee mun show boo show sheen yoong kah;* Do you accept credit cards?)

- ✔ **Yǒu méiyǒu shāngwù zhōngxīn?** (*yo mayo shahng woo joong sheen;* Is there a business center?)

- ✔ **Nǐmen de fángjiān yǒu méiyǒu wǎngluò lián-jié?** (*nee mun duh fahng jyan yo mayo wahng lwaw lyan jyeh;* Do your rooms have Internet access?)

You have many kinds of rooms to choose from, depending on your budget and your unique needs:

- ✔ **yíge ānjìng de fángjiān** (*ee guh ahn jeeng duh fahng jyan;* a quiet room)

- ✔ **yíge guāngxiàn hǎo de fángjiān** (*ee guh gwahng shyan how duh fahng jyan;* a bright room)

- ✔ **yíge cháo hǎi de fángjiān** (*ee guh chaow hi duh fahng jyan;* a room with an ocean view)

- ✔ **yíge cháo yuànzi de fángjiān** (*ee guh chaow ywan dzuh duh fahng jyan;* a room facing the courtyard)

- ✔ **yíge yǒu kōngtiáo de fángjiān** (*ee guh yo koong tyaow duh fahng jyan;* a room with air conditioning)

- ✔ **yíge dài yángtái de fángjiān** (*ee guh dye yahng tye duh fahng jyan;* a room with a balcony)

- ✔ **yíge bù xǐyān de fángjiān** (*ee guh boo she yan duh fahng jyan;* a nonsmoking room)

- ✔ **yíge fāngbiàn cánjí rén de fángjiān** (*ee guh fahng byan tsahn jee run duh fahng jyan;* a room equipped for handicapped people)

Words to Know

dāi	dye	to stay
dānrén fángjiān	dahn run fahng jyan	single room
dōu	doe	both; all
dōu yíyàng the same	doe ee yahng	they're both
hé	huh	and
		continued

Words to Know *(continued)*

jiàgé	jyah guh	price
shuāngrén fángjiān	shwahng run fahng jyan	double room
tàojiān	taow jyan	suite
yígòng	ee goong	altogether
yíyàng	ee yahng	the same

The coverb **hé** (*huh;* and), along with the noun that always follows it, precedes the main verb or adjective of a sentence. Some synonyms of **hé** are **gēn** (*gun*), **yǔ** (*yew*), and **tóng** (*toong*), although **tóng** translates more closely to "with."

Checking In Before You Hit the Pool

Aaahhh, **Yàzhōu** (*yah joe;* Asia)! Its allure often begins as soon as you pull up to the front entrance and walk through the hotel door. You may even find yourself mysteriously lingering a bit in the **dàtīng** (*dah teeng;* lobby), visually casing the joint long enough to take in all sorts of amenities. The luxuries at your disposal may include the following:

- **diànshì** (*dyan shir;* television)
- **gānxǐ fúwù** (*gahn she foo woo;* dry cleaning)
- **huíyā ànmóchí** (*hway yah ahn maw chir;* hot tub)
- **lǚguǎn fàndiàn** (*lyew gwahn fahn dyan;* hotel restaurant)
- **shāngwù zhōngxīn** (*shahng woo joong sheen;* business center)

- ✔ **tǐyùguǎn** (*tee yew gwahn;* gym)
- ✔ **yóuyǒngchí** (*yo yoong chir;* swimming pool)

Before you can take advantage of these conveniences, however, you have to officially **bànlǐ rùzhù shǒuxù** (*bahn lee roo joo show shyew;* check in). You don't want to be caught red handed running in the **tǐyùguǎn** or relaxing in the **huíyā ànmōchí** unless you're a bona fide guest, right?

When you walk up to the **fàndiàn qiántái** (*fahn dyan chyan tye;* reception desk), you'll invariably find yourself needing to say one of the following sentences:

- ✔ **Wǒ yǐjīng yùdìng le fángjiān.** (*waw ee jeeng yew deeng luh fahng jyan;* I already made a reservation.)
- ✔ **Wǒ méiyǒu yùdìng fángjiān.** (*waw mayo yew deeng fahng jyan;* I don't have a reservation.)
- ✔ **Nǐmen hái yǒu fángjiān ma?** (*nee mun hi yo fahng jyan mah;* Do you have any rooms available?)

If you're in luck, the hotel will have at least one **kōng** (*koong;* empty, vacant) **fángjiān** (*fahng jyan;* room). If the hotel has no available space, you'll hear

Duìbùqǐ, wǒmen kèmǎn le. (*dway boo chee, waw mun kuh mahn luh;* Sorry, there are no vacancies/we're full.)

In this case, you may need these phrases:

- ✔ **Zāogāo! Nǐ néng bù néng tuījiàn biéde lǚguǎn?** (*dzaow gaow. nee nung boo nung tway jyan byeh duh lyew gwahn;* Rats! Could you perhaps recommend another hotel then?)
- ✔ **Kéyǐ. Gébì de lǚguǎn yǒu kōng fángjiān. Nǐ zuì hǎo zǒu guò qù shì shì kàn.** (*kuh yee. guh bee duh lyew gwahn yo koong fahng jyan. nee dzway how dzoe gwaw chyew shir shir kahn;* Yes. The hotel next door has vacancies. You may as well walk over there and have a look.)

The **qiántái fúwùyuán** (*chyan tye foo woo ywan;* front desk clerk) will ask you to **tián** (*tyan;* fill out) a couple of **biǎo** (*byaow;* forms) to book your room, so have a **gāngbǐ** (*gahng bee;* pen) and some form of **zhèngjiàn** (*juhng jyan;* ID) ready — especially your **hùzhào** (*hoo jaow;* passport). Voilà! You're officially a hotel **kèrén** (*kuh run;* guest).

After you successfully manage to check in, a **xínglǐyuán** (*sheeng lee ywan;* porter/bell boy) immediately appears to help take your **xínglǐ** (*sheeng lee;* luggage) to your **fángjiān**. After he lets you in, he'll give you the **yàoshi** (*yaow shir;* key) if you didn't get it from the **qiántái fúwùyuán** downstairs.

Now you can finally **xiūxi** (*shyo she;* take a rest) and maybe fall asleep. Before you do, however, you may want to put in for a wake-up call. All you have to say is

> **Qǐng nǐ jiào wǒ qǐchuáng.** (*cheeng nee jyaow waw chee chwahng; literally:* Please call me to get out of bed.)

Words to Know

biéde	byeh duh	other
duìbùqǐ	dway boo chee	I'm sorry
gébì	guh bee	next door
lǚguǎn	lyew gwahn	hotel
tuījiàn	tway jyan	recommend
zāogāo	dzaow gaow	rats!/what a shame

Taking Advantage of Hotel Service

You're finally ensconced in your big, beautiful hotel room when you discover that the **mén suǒ bú shàng** (*mun swaw boo shahng;* door doesn't lock) and the **kōngtiáo huài le** (*koong tyaow hwye luh;* air conditioning doesn't work). To make matters worse, your **chuānghu dǎ bù kāi** (*chwahng hoo dah boo kye;* window won't open). Heat wave! It may be hard to believe, but in addition to all that, your **mǎtǒng dǔzhùle** (*mah toong doo joo luh;* toilet is clogged). Time to call the nearest **kèfáng fúwùyuán** (*kuh fahng foo woo ywan;* hotel housekeeper) and ask for help.

You may want the **kèfáng fúwùyuán** to **sòng** (*soong;* send) the following items right over:

- ✔ **chuīfēngjī** (*chway fung jee;* hair dryer)
- ✔ **máojīn** (*maow jeen;* towel)
- ✔ **máotǎn** (*maow tahn;* blanket)
- ✔ **wèishēngzhǐ** (*way shung jir;* toilet paper)
- ✔ **zhěntóu** (*jun toe;* pillow)

Quickly call if the following pieces of equipment are **huàile** (*hwye luh;* broken) and need immediate fixing:

- ✔ **chāzuò** (*chah dzwaw;* electric outlet)
- ✔ **kāiguān** (*kye gwahn;* light switch)
- ✔ **kōngtiáo** (*koong tyaow;* air conditioner)
- ✔ **mǎtǒng** (*mah toong;* toilet)
- ✔ **nuǎnqì** (*nwan chee;* heater)
- ✔ **yáokòng qì** (*yaow koong chee;* remote control)

Maybe you just need someone to **dǎsǎo fángjiān** (*dah saow fahng jyan;* clean the room). Oh well. Even the best hotels need some tweaking every now and then.

You interact with many different employees on any given hotel stay:

- **fúwùtái jīnglǐ** (*foo woo tye jeeng lee;* concierge)
- **fúwùyuán** (*foo woo ywan;* attendant)
- **fúwùyuán lǐngbān** (*foo woo ywan leeng bahn;* bell captain)
- **zhùlǐ jīnglǐ** (*joo lee jeeng lee;* assistant manager)
- **zǒngjīnglǐ** (*dzoong jeeng lee;* general manager)

Before you decide to order room service, however, just remember that it's often **guì liǎng bèi** (*gway lyahng bay;* twice as expensive) as dining in the **lǚguǎn fàndiàn** (*lyew gwahn fahn dyan;* hotel restaurant), because the service is more **fāngbiàn** (*fahng byan;* convenient).

Here's a practice conversation:

Housekeeper: **Kèfáng fúwùyuán!** (*kuh fahng foo woo ywan;* Housekeeping!)

David: **Qǐng jìn!** (*cheeng jin;* Come on in!)

Housekeeper: **Yǒu shénme wèntí?** (*yo shummuh one tee;* What seems to be the trouble?)

David: **Zhèige shuǐlóngtóu huàile. Yě méiyǒu rèshuǐ.** (*jay guh shway loong toe hwye luh. yeah mayo ruh shway;* This faucet is broken. There's also no hot water.)

Housekeeper: **Hěn duìbùqǐ. Mǎshàng sòng shuǐnuǎngōng guòlái kànkàn.** (*hun dway boo chee. mah shahng soong shway nwan goong gwaw lye kahn kahn;* I'm so sorry. We'll send a plumber right away to have a look.)

David: **Xiǎojiě, nǐmen yǒu méiyǒu xǐyī fúwù?** (*shyaow jyeh, nee men yo mayo she ee foo woo;* Miss, do you have any laundry service?)

Housekeeper: **Yǒu.** (*yo;* Yes we do.)

David: **Hǎo jíle. Jīntiān kěyǐ bǎ zhè xiē yīfú xǐ hǎo ma?** (*how jee luh. jin tyan kuh yee bah jay shyeh ee foo she how mah;* Great. Can I have these clothes cleaned today?)

To make a comparison by saying that something is a number of times more expensive than something else, you first use the word **guì** (*gway;* expensive), followed by the number of times you think it's more expensive and the word **bèi** (*bay;* roughly translated as "times"). You can compare the relative cost of two products or services by using the word **bǐ** (*bee;* compared to) in the following pattern:

X **bǐ** Y **guì** # **bèi**

Here are some examples:

✔ **Zuò chūzūchē bǐ zuò gōnggòng qìchē guì wǔ bèi.** (*zwaw choo dzoo chuh bee dzwaw goong goong chee chuh gway woo bay;* Taking a cab is five times more expensive than taking the bus.)

✔ **Zhèitiáo qúnzi bǐ nèige guì shí bèi.** (*jay tyaow chwun dzuh bee nay guh gway shir bay;* This skirt is ten times more expensive than that one.)

Every hotel room in China has a large flask of boiling water that you can use to make tea or for drinking water. Never drink directly from the tap. You can brush your teeth with tap water because you just spit it out. Local Chinese don't dare drink the tap water either, so you're in good company.

Words to Know

mǎshàng	mah shahng	immediately
méi wèntí	may one tee	no problem
qùdiào	chyew dyaow	erase; remove
		continued

Words to Know (continued)

qǐng jìn	cheeng jin	come in, please
shuǐnuǎngōng	shway nwan goong	plumber
wūdiǎn	woo dyan	stain
xǐ	she	to wash
xǐyī fúwù	she ee foo woo	laundry service
yóuqíshì	yo chee shir	especially

Checking Out Before Heading Out

Time to **téngchū** (*tuhng choo;* vacate) your hotel **fángjiān** (*fahng jyan;* room) and **tuìfáng** (*tway fahng;* check out).

You may need to say some of the following as you begin the end of your stay:

- ✔ **Wǒ yào fù zhàng.** (*waw yaow foo jahng;* I'd like to pay the bill.)
- ✔ **Nǐmen jiēshòu shénme xìnyòng kǎ?** (*nee mun jyeh show shummuh sheen yoong kah;* Which credit cards do you accept?)
- ✔ **Zhè búshì wǒde zhāngdàn.** (*jay boo shir waw duh jahng dahn;* This isn't my bill.)
- ✔ **Wǒ bù yīnggāi fù zhè xiàng.** (*waw boo eeng gye foo jay shyahng;* I shouldn't be charged for this.)

✔ **Jiézhàng yǐhòu wǒ néng bùnéng bǎ bāoguǒ liú zài qiántái?** (*jyeh jahng ee ho waw nung boo nung bah baow gwaw lyo dzye chyan tye;* After checking out, may I leave my bags at the front desk?)

✔ **Yǒu méiyǒu qù fēijīchǎng de bānchē?** (*yo mayo chyew fay jee chahng duh ban chuh;* Is there a shuttle to the airport?)

Words to Know

fángjià	fahng jya	room charge
jié zhàng	jyeh jahng	figure out the bill
suǒyǐ	swaw yee	so; therefore
tuìfáng	tway fahng	check out
yàoshi	yaow shir	key
zhàngdān	jahng dahn	bill

Chapter 11

Dealing with Emergencies

- -

In This Chapter

▶ Yelling for help

▶ Visiting your doctor

▶ Going to the authorities

▶ Looking for legal advice

- -

*T*his chapter gives you the language tools you need to communicate your problems during your times of need — whether you need a doctor, the police, or an attorney.

Calling for Help in Times of Need

When you're faced with an emergency, you don't want to waste your time searching for an oversized Chinese-English dictionary to figure out how to quickly call for help. Try memorizing these phrases before a situation arises:

▶ **Jiù mìng!** (*jyo meeng;* Help; Save me!)

▶ **Zhuā zéi!** (*jwah dzay;* Stop, thief!)

▶ **Zháohuǒ la!** (*jaow hwaw lah;* Fire!)

▶ **Jiào jiùhùchē!** (*jyaow jyo hoo chuh;* Call an ambulance!)

▶ **Jiào jǐngchá!** (*jyaow jeeng chah;* Call the police!)

Be careful when you say the words **jiào** (*jyaow;* to call) and **jiù** (*jyo;* to save) in the previous phrases. You don't want to mistakenly ask someone to save the police when you want him to call the police.

Sometimes you have to ask for someone who speaks English. Here are some phrases you can quickly blurt out during emergencies:

- ✔ **Nǐ shuō Yīngwén ma?** (*nee shwaw eeng one mah;* Do you speak English?)

- ✔ **Wǒ xūyào yíge jiǎng Yīngwén de lǜshī.** (*waw shyew yaow ee guh jyahng eeng one duh lyew shir;* I need a lawyer who speaks English.)

- ✔ **Yǒu méiyǒu jiǎng Yīngwén de dàifu?** (*yo mayo jyahng eeng one duh dye foo;* Are there any English-speaking doctors?)

When you finally get someone on the phone who can help you, you need to know what to say to get immediate help:

- ✔ **Wǒ bèi rén qiǎng le.** (*waw bay run chyahng luh;* I've been robbed.)

- ✔ **Yǒu rén shòu shāng le.** (*yo run show shahng luh;* People are injured.)

- ✔ **Wǒ yào huì bào yíge chē huò.** (*waw yaow hway baow ee guh chuh hwaw;* I'd like to report a car accident.)

Receiving Medical Care

If you suddenly find yourself in the **yīyuàn** (*ee ywan;* hospital) or otherwise visiting an **yīshēng** (*ee shung;* doctor), you need to explain what ails you — often in a hurry. Use Table 11-1 to figure out how to say the basic body parts.

Table 11-1	Basic Body Parts	
Chinese Word	*Pronunciation*	*English Word*
shēntǐ	shun tee	body
gēbō	guh baw	arm
jiānbǎng	jyan bahng	shoulder
shǒu	show	hand
shǒuzhǐ	show jir	finger
tuǐ	tway	leg
jiǎo	jyaow	foot
tóu	toe	head
bózi	baw dzuh	neck
xiōng	shyoong	chest
bèi	bay	back
liǎn	lyan	face
yǎnjīng	yan jeeng	eye
ěrduō	are dwaw	ear
bízi	bee dzuh	nose
hóulóng	ho loong	throat
gǔtóu	goo toe	bone
jīròu	jee row	muscles
shénjīng	shun jeeng	nerves
fèi	fay	lungs
gān	gahn	liver
shèn	shun	kidney
xīn	shin	heart
dùzi	doo dzuh	stomach

Finding a doctor

If your **yùnqì** (*yewn chee;* luck) is good, you'll never need to use any of the phrases I present in this chapter. If you end up running **dǎoméi** (*daow may;* out of luck), however, keep reading. Even if you've never **chōuyān** (*cho yan;* smoked) a day in your life, you can still develop **késòu** (*kuh so;* a cough) or even **qìguǎnyán** (*chee gwahn yan;* bronchitis). Time to see an **yīshēng** (*ee shung;* doctor). The following is a sample dialog between a nurse and patient.

> Nurse: **Nǐ zěnme bùshūfú?** (*nee dzummah boo shoo foo;* What's wrong?)
>
> Patient: **Wǒ gǎnjué bùshūfú kěshì bù zhīdào wǒ déle shénme bìng.** (*waw gahn jweh boo shoo foo kuh shir boo jir daow waw duh luh shummuh beeng;* I don't feel well, but I don't know what I have.)
>
> Nurse: **Nǐ fā shāo ma?** (*nee fah shaow mah;* Are you running a fever?)
>
> Patient: **Méiyǒu, dànshì wǒ tóuyūn. Yěxǔ wǒ xūyào kàn nèikē yīshēng.** (*mayo, dahn shir waw toe yewn. yeh shyew waw shyew yaow kahn nay kuh ee shung;* No, but I feel dizzy. Perhaps I need to see an internist.)

Words to Know

bìngrén	beeng run	patient
hùshi	hoo shir	nurse
kànbìng	kahn beeng	to see a doctor
yáyī	yah ee	dentist
yīshēng	ee shung	doctor

Describing what ails you

Whether you make a sudden trip to the **jízhěnshì** (*jee jun shir;* emergency room) or take a normal visit to a doctor's office, you'll probably be asked

> **Yǒu shénme zhèngzhuàng?** (*yo shummuh juhng jwahng;* What sorts of symptoms do you have?*)

Table 11-2 lists some symptoms you may have.

Table 11-2	Common Medical Symptoms	
Chinese Phrase	*Pronunciation*	*English Phrase*
pàngle	pahng luh	put on weight
shòule	show luh	lose weight
fāshāo	fah shaow	to have a fever
lādùzi	lah doo dzuh	diarrhea
biànmì	byan mee	constipation
ěxīn	uh sheen	nauseous
hóulóng téng	ho loong tung	sore throat
tóu téng	toe tung	headache
wèi téng	way tung	stomach ache
bèi téng	bay tung	back ache
ěr téng	are tung	ear ache
yá téng	yah tung	tooth ache
xiàntǐ zhǒngle	shyan tee joong luh	swollen glands

Your doctor has a laundry list of inspections she must perform when you hit the check-up table:

> ✓ **Qǐng juǎnqǐ nǐde xiùzi.** (*cheeng jwan chee nee duh shyo dzuh;* Please roll up your sleeve.)

✔ **Wǒ yòng tīngzhěnqì tīng yíxià nǐde xīnzàng.** (*waw yoong teeng jun chee teeng ee shyah nee duh shin dzahng;* I'm going to use a stethoscope to listen to your heart.)

✔ **Shēn hūxī.** (*shun hoo she;* Take a deep breath.)

✔ **Bǎ zuǐ zhāngkāi.** (*bah dzway jahng kye;* Open your mouth.)

✔ **Bǎ shétóu shēn chūlái.** (*bah shuh toe shun choo lye;* Stick out your tongue.)

✔ **Wǒmen huàyàn yíxià xiǎobiàn.** (*waw men hwah yan ee shyah shyaow byan;* Let's have your urine tested.)

The following phrases about insurance may come in handy:

✔ **Yǒu méiyǒu yīliáo bǎoxiǎn?** (*yo mayo ee lyaow baow shyan;* Do you have any medical insurance?)

✔ **Hǎo. Qǐng tián yíxià zhèi zhāng biǎo.** (*how. cheeng tyan ee shyah jay jahng byaow;* Alright. Please fill out this form.)

Words to Know

bìnglì	beeng lee	medical history
bìngle	beeng luh	to be sick
bìngrén	beeng run	patient
fāyán	fah yan	an infection
gǎnmào	gahn maow	to have a cold
gāo xuěyā	gaow shweh yah	high blood pressure

jiǎnchá	jyan chah	to examine
liúgǎn	lyo gahn	the flu
shòushāng	show shahng	be injured
wǒ bùshūfu	waw boo shoo foo	I don't feel well
zháoliáng	jaow lyahng	to catch a cold

Discussing your medical history

When you see a doctor for the first time, he or she will want to find out about your **bìng shǐ** (*beeng shir;* medical history). You may hear the following query:

Nǐ jiā yǒu méiyǒu ____ de bìnglì? (*nee jyah yo mayo ___ duh beeng lee;* Does your family have any history of ___?)

Table 11-3 lists some of the more serious illnesses that I hope neither you nor your family members have ever had.

Table 11-3	Serious Illnesses	
Chinese Word(s)	*Pronunciation*	*English Word(s)*
áizhèng	eye juhng	cancer
àizībìng	eye dzuh beeng	AIDS
bǐngxíng gānyán	beeng sheeng gahn yan	hepatitis C
fèi jiéhé	fay jyeh huh	tuberculosis
fèi'ái	fay eye	lung cancer
huòluàn	hwaw lwan	cholera

(continued)

Table 11-3 *(continued)*

Chinese Word(s)	Pronunciation	English Word(s)
jiǎxíng gānyán	jya sheeng gahn yan	hepatitis A
lìjí	lee jee	dysentery
qìchuánbìng	chee chwan beeng	asthma
shuǐdòu	shway doe	chicken pox
tángniàobìng	tahng nyaow beeng	diabetes
xīnzàng yǒu máobìng	shin dzahng yo maow beeng	heart trouble
yǐxíng gānyán	ee sheeng gahn yan	hepatitis B
yǒu lìjí	yo lee jee	dysentery

Making a diagnosis

You may have heard stories about how doctors who use traditional medical techniques from ancient cultures can just take one look at a person and immediately know what ails him or her. The truth is, aside from simple colds and the flu, most doctors still need to take all kinds of tests to give a proper diagnosis. They may even need to perform the following tasks:

- ✔ **huà yàn** (*hwah yan;* lab tests)
- ✔ **xīndiàntú** (*shin dyan too;* electrocardiogram)
- ✔ **huàyàn yíxià xiǎobiàn** (*hwah yan ee shyah shyaow byan;* have your urine tested)

Here are some other phrases you may hear:

- ✔ **Nǐde tǐwēn zhèngcháng.** (*nee duh tee one juhng chahng;* Your temperature is normal.)
- ✔ **Kěyǐ chuánrǎn ma?** (*kuh yee chwahn rahn mah;* Is it contagious?)

> ✔ **Yánzhòng ma?** (*yan joong mah;* Is it serious?)
>
> ✔ **Tā děi zài chuángshàng tǎng duōjiǔ?** (*tah day dzye chwahng shahng tahng dwaw jyo;* How long must she rest in bed?)

When you give approximate numbers or amounts, you don't need to use the word "or" (**huò zhe**)," as in "three or four days." Just say the numbers right after each other to automatically imply the "or." For example, **wǔ liù ge rén** (*woo lyo guh run*) means five or six people, and **sì wǔ tiān** (*suh woo tyan*) means four or five days.

Words to Know

chōu xiě	cho shyeh	to draw blood
dàbiàn	dah byan	to have a bowel movement
liáng tǐwēn	lyahng tee one	take one's temperature
màibó	my baw	pulse
wēndù jì	one doo jee	thermometer
xiǎobiàn	shyaow byan	to urinate
xiě/xuè	shyeh/shweh	blood
xuèyā	shweh yah	blood pressure

Treating yourself to better health

Not everything can be cured with a bowl of **jī tāng** (*jee tahng;* chicken soup), despite what my grandmother told me. Your doctor may prescribe some **yào** (*yaow;*

medicine) to make you feel better. After you **ná** (*nah;* fill) your **yào** (*yaow;* prescription), you may find the following instructions on the bottle:

- ✔ **Nín néng bùnéng gěi wǒ zhuā zhèige yào?** (*neen nung boo nung gay waw jwah jay guh yaow;* Can you fill this prescription for me?)

- ✔ **Wǒ duì qīngméisù yǒu guòmǐn.** (*waw dway cheeng may soo yo gwaw meen;* I'm allergic to penicillin.)

- ✔ **Wǒ yě yào zhì késòu de yào.** (*waw yeah yaow jir kuh so duh yaow;* I'd also like something for a cough.)

- ✔ **Měi sìge xiǎoshí chī yícì.** (*may suh guh shyaow shir chir ee tsuh;* Take one tablet every four hours.)

- ✔ **Měi tiān chī liǎng cì, měi cì sān piàn.** (*may tyan chir lyahng tsuh, may tsuh sahn pyan;* Take three tablets, twice a day.)

- ✔ **Fàn hòu chī.** (*fahn ho chir;* Take after eating.)

Words to Know

āsīpǐlín	ah suh pee leen	aspirin
chī yào	chir yaow	to take medicine
dānjià	dahn jya	stretcher
dǎ zhēn	dah juhn	injection
dòng shǒushù	doong show shoo	to undergo an operation
jiùhùchē	jyo hoo chuh	ambulance
jízhěnshì	jee juhn shir	emergency room

kàngshēngsù	kahng shung soo	antibiotics
kàngsuānyào	kahng swan yaow	antacid
wàikē	why kuh	surgery
wéitāmìng	way tah meeng	vitamin
Xī yào	she yaow	Western medicine
yào	yaow	medicine
yàofáng	yaow fahng	pharmacy
yàowán	yaow wahn	pill
yīyuàn	ee ywan	hospital
zhēnjiǔ	juhn jyo	acupuncture
zhěnliáosuǒ	juhn lyaow swaw	clinic
Zhōng yào	joong yaow	Chinese medicine

Calling the Police

Have you ever had your pocketbook **tōu le** (*toe luh;* stolen)? Being a victim is an awful feeling, and I know from personal experience. You feel **shēngqì** (*shung chee;* angry) at such a **kěpà** (*kuh pah;* scary) experience, especially if it happens in another country and the **zéi** (*dzay;* thief) **táopǎo** (*taow paow;* escapes) quickly.

You always need to be prepared with some key words you can use when the **jǐngchá** (*jeeng chah;* police) finally pull up in the **jǐngchē** (*jeeng chuh;* police car) and take you back to the **jǐngchájú** (*jeeng chah jyew;*

police station) to identify a potential **zéi**. Hopefully the culprit will be **zhuā zháo le** (*jwah jaow luh;* arrested).

You may also find yourself in an emergency that doesn't involve you. If you ever witness an accident, here are some phrases you can relay to the police or emergency workers:

- ✔ **Tā bèi qìchē yà zháo le.** (*tah bay chee chuh yah jaow luh;* He was run over by a car.)

- ✔ **Tā zài liúxiě.** (*tah dzye lyo shyeh;* He's bleeding.)

- ✔ **Bié kū. Jǐngchá hé jiùhùchē láile.** (*byeh koo. jeeng chah huh jyo hoo chuh lye luh;* Don't cry. The police and the ambulance have arrived.)

Acquiring Legal Help

Nine out of ten foreigners never need to look for a lawyer during a stay in China, which isn't as litigious a society as the United States, to be sure. If you do need a **lǜshī** (*lyew shir;* lawyer), however, your best bet is to check with your country's **dàshǐguǎn** (*dah shir gwahn;* embassy) or **lǐnshìguǎn** (*leen shir gwahn;* consulate) for advice.

It can be very **máf an** (*mah fun;* annoying) and stressful to have to deal with **lǜshī**, no matter what country you're in, but you have to admit — they do know the **fǎlǜ** (*fah lyew;* law). And if you have to go to **fǎyuàn** (*fah ywan;* court) for any serious **shìjiàn** (*shir jyan;* incident), you want the judge to **pànjué** (*pahn jweh;* make a decision) in your favor. Moral of the story: Good **lǜshī** are worth their weight in **jīn** (*gin;* gold), even if you still consider them **shāyú** (*shah yew;* sharks) in the end.

Chapter 12

Ten Favorite Chinese Expressions

● ●

*T*his chapter offers some idiomatic expressions that make you sound like a native. You hear these expressions all the time in typical daily situations.

Gōngxǐ Gōngxǐ

goong she goong she; Congratulations!

You say **gōngxǐ gōngxǐ** for happy occasions when congratulations are in order.

"My wife just had a baby!" your friend says. "Wow! I didn't even know she was pregnant," you say. **"Gōngxǐ gōngxǐ!"**

Hey! You just turned 21. Now you can finally go to a bar. **Gōngxǐ gōngxǐ!** Let's go!

 On the Chinese New Year, you hear not only **"gōngxǐ gōngxǐ,"** but also **"gōngxǐ fācái"** (*goong she fah tsye*), which means "Congratulations and may you prosper."

Yí Lù Píng'ān

ee loo peeng ahn; Bon Voyage! Have a good trip.

This phrase is great to use when a friend or acquaintance is about to embark on a long journey. When you see someone off at the airport, you hear many people say this phrase. You may want to teach your family and friends **yí lù píng'ān** before you board the plane!

Yì Yán Nán Jìn

ee yan nahn jeen; It's a long story.

Maybe someone wants to know how you got that black eye. Maybe you don't really want to go into the details. Just say **yì yán nán jìn** to save the blow-by-blow description for when you're ready.

Mămă Hūhū

mah mah hoo hoo; So-so

The phrase **mămă hūhū** literally means "horse horse tiger tiger." You use this expression when you want to indicate a situation is just okay or mediocre.

Kāi Wán Xiào

kye (rhymes with pie) *wahn shyaow;* Just kidding, or You've got to be kidding!

You say **kāi wán xiào** when you can't believe your ears. Suppose your coworker just told you she's been fired, even though she was promoted only a month ago. That definitely calls for a **kāi wán xiào** in response. When she finally tells you it's not true, she adds **kāi wán xiào** at the end. She was just kidding. (Now you're really angry.)

Máfan Nǐ

mah fahn nee; Sorry to trouble you.

You say **máfan nǐ** when, although you don't want to put anyone out, you politely accept an extended offer to do something for you. If you can't reach the salt at the other end of the dinner table and someone offers to pass it to you, you say **máfan nǐ.** It means, "So sorry to trouble you, but would you mind?"

Zěnme Yàng?

dzummah yahng; How's it going, or what's up?

A great catchall expression when you run into old friends and want to find out how they've been or what they're up to these days. You just say: Hey! **Zěnme yàng?**

 Another way you can use **zěnme** is by adding **"le"** in place of **"yàng"** at the end. **(Nǐ zěnme le?)** If you do, you say, "Hey, what's wrong with you?" Kind of like, "What could you possibly have been thinking when you did such a stupid thing?"

Qǐng Wèn

cheeng one; Please, may I ask; excuse me, but . . .

Before you ask a question, be polite and preface it with **qǐng wèn.** You're asking if you can even ask about something. You can use it when you go shopping and need to address a store clerk:

Qǐng wèn (Please, may I ask), how much is that thousand-year-old egg?

You can also use it when you need directions and have to approach a total stranger:

Qǐng wèn (Excuse me), which bus can take me to the Temple of Heaven?

Zìjǐ Lái

dzuh gee lye; I'll help myself, thanks.

The rules of Chinese eating etiquette dictate that you should never start to fill up your plate before at least attempting to serve someone else first. **Zìjǐ lái** is a polite expression you use to indicate that you can help yourself as soon as someone starts to serve you. A host always starts to serve the guests sitting closest, but the guests should always say **zìjǐ lái** (and then relent and let the person serve them anyway) for each and every course. After the host has started a dish, however, you may indeed begin to serve yourself.

Āiya!

eye yah; Oh my!

Āiya can be heard all over China whenever people feel frustrated, shocked, or even just plain old annoyed. You hear it when you show up to your parents' home for dinner with a friend who looks like he's in a punk rock band. You may even say it yourself when you realize you left your briefcase in the taxi, which is now halfway across town.

Chapter 13

Ten Phrases That Make You Sound Like a Local

• •

*T*his chapter gives you phrases that help your conversation for many social occasions. Notice that the Chinese often repeat phrases. Repeating words happens often in spoken Chinese.

Huānyíng Huānyíng!

hwan yeeng hwan yeeng; Welcome!

Use this phrase when guests arrive at your home or in your country to make them feel at home. And if you say **huānyíng zài lái** (*hwan yeeng dzye lye*) before they leave, it means you welcome them to come again.

Bǐcǐ Bǐcǐ

bee tsuh bee tsuh; same to you; you too

This little phrase comes in handy when someone wishes you well or gives you a compliment that merits return so you don't appear vain. What's that you say? Great looking dress I have on? **Bǐcǐ bǐcǐ.** (Yours looks great, too.)

Jiŭyăng Jiŭyăng

jyoe yahng jyoe yahng; Pleased to meet you; *literally:* I have admired you for a long time.

Saying **Jiŭyăng jiŭyăng** when you first meet someone you've heard something about is a polite gesture.

Màn Màn Chī!

mahn mahn chir; Bon Appetit!

Be sure to say **màn màn chī!** to the others at your table before you take your first bite. You'll win hearts all around. It actually means "eat real slowly." This phrase lets everyone know you hope they take their time and enjoy the meal.

Wŏ Qĭng Kè

waw cheeng kuh; It's on me; My treat.

You hear this phrase day in and day out all over China. Everyone wants to be the one to pay the bill, so folks make a big deal out of being the first person to go to the hip when the check comes.

Friends often make a joke by adding **"nĭ fù qián"** (*nee foo chyan*) at the end of this phrase. If you hear someone say **"wŏ qĭng kè, nĭ fù qián,"** it means "I'll take the bill, but you'll be the one to pay it." Only say this when you dine with a good friend who can take a joke.

Yŏu Kōng Lái Wán

yo koong lye wahn; Please come again.

Just before guests leave your home, say **"Yŏu kōng lái wán."** (*literally:* When you have time, come back and play.) Sometimes you also hear people say **"màn**

zǒu," (*mahn dzoe*) which literally means "walk slowly" and is loosely translated as "careful going home."

Láojià Láojià

laow jyah laow jyah; excuse me; pardon me

Ever wonder what to say when you need to pass a person who's standing in your way? **Láojià láojià** is the phrase you want to remember for crowded moments. It offers you a nice way of getting someone's attention without being rude.

Zhù Nǐ Zǎo Rì Kāng Fù

joo nee dzaow ir kahng foo; Get well soon.

Ideally you won't have to use this expression too often, but if you do, at least the folks hearing it will know your colloquial Chinese is good.

Búkèqi

boo kuh chee; you're welcome; no problem; don't mention it

You say **búkèqi** as the bookend to **xièxiè** (*shyeh shyeh;* thanks). You can't say one without expecting to hear the other. **Búkèqi** represents more than just a response to "thank you," however. It's part and parcel of a larger group of words that express a humble spirit, which the Chinese always treasure in friends and acquaintances. If someone thanks you profusely for something you do, whether big or small, never accept the thanks as something you agree you deserve. Giving yourself a pat on the back is the opposite of what you want to convey. Always make it sound like your deed is no big deal, something you prefer to downplay.

Hǎo Jiǔ Méi Jiàn

how jyoe may jyan; long time no see

You can use this phrase in all seriousness or in jest if you've just seen someone an hour before. Either way, it puts people in a good mood to know that you care about being in their presence again.

Index

Notes

....

_____

_____

_____

_____

_____

_____

_____

_____

_____

_____

_____

_____

_____

_____

_____

_____

_____

Notes

Notes

....

Notes

Notes

Notes

....

_____

_____

_____

_____

_____

_____

_____

_____

_____

_____

_____

_____

_____

_____

_____

_____

Notes

....

Notes

....

_____

_____

_____

_____

_____

_____

_____

_____

_____

_____

_____

_____

_____

_____

_____

_____

_____

Notes